Management:
A Biblical Approach

Myron D. Rush

Run So That You May Win.
ivictor.com

Victor is an imprint of
Cook Communications Ministries, Colorado Springs, Colorado 80918
Cook Communications, Paris, Ontario
Kingsway Communications, Eastbourne, England

MANAGEMENT: A BIBLICAL APPROACH
© 2002 by Myron Rush

First Printing, 1983, SP Publications
Printed in the United States of America

1 2 3 4 5 6 7 8 9 10 Printing/Year 06 05 04 03 02

Editor: Craig Bubeck, Sr. Editor
Cover Design: Buffalo Creative
Interior Design: Buffalo Creative

Library of Congress Cataloging-in-Publication Data

Rush, Myron (Myron D.)
    Management, a biblical approach / by Myron Rush.
      p. cm.
Originally published: Wheaton, Ill. : Victor Books, c1983.
    ISBN 0-7814-3745-8
    1. Management--Religious aspects--Christianity. 2. Christianity. I. Title.
    HD38 .R845 2002
    658--dc21
                                    2001005712

Contents

ABOUT THE AUTHOR

Myron D. Rush is founder and president of Management Training Systems, a consulting firm specializing in tailor-made training and consulting services for business firms and Christian organizations. He is also co-owner of Sunlight Industries, Inc., a solar energy manufacturing firm.

Mr. Rush is the author of *Tapping Employee Creativity*, which deals with the participative management process in private industry. He travels throughout the United States conducting management seminars and consulting sessions that focus on applying biblical principles of management.

Mr. Rush has an extensive background in management. He has served numerous corporations and federal agencies as a management consultant, including the Department of Health, Education, and Welfare in Washington, D.C.

Mr. Rush earned a master's degree in social science and education from Central Missouri State University. He has taught various management and supervisory courses for Mesa College's Department of Continuing Education, the College of Eastern Utah, and Navajo Community College.

Myron makes his home in Colorado Springs, Colorado with his wife, Lorraine, and his two children, Delphine and Ron.

PREFACE

As a management consultant, seminar speaker, and co-owner of a manufacturing firm, I have observed firsthand the growing need for strong leadership and management both within the business community and within our Christian organizations. Modern technological advancements coupled with the numerous pressures associated with unstable economic conditions are making leaders in both fields aware of the need to improve their management skills.

However, Christians are discovering that the secular philosophy of management and leadership often conflicts with their Christian values. Many Christian leaders are looking for an alternative approach to management. The objective of this book is to provide such an alternative.

I have attempted to focus on biblical principles of organizational leadership and management. I have tried to present the various tools of management required in developing and maintaining a successful business or Christian organization, and to present their biblical bases.

In some respects, this has been a difficult book to write. I have attempted to speak to the Christian businessperson wanting to operate and manage his secular business from a biblical perspective. At the same time, I have addressed the leader in the Christian organization. Certainly, most of the principles apply to both situations.

This is not a book on how to become a more spiritual leader—though I will be delighted if readers develop more spiritual maturity as a result of reading it. The focus of the book, however, is on how to lead people and manage organizations and businesses from a biblical viewpoint.

I have attempted to emphasize the practical rather than the philosophical aspects of leadership and management. Instead of citing hypothetical management and business situations, I have presented numerous real organizational and individual successes and failures taken from my personal files. However, both individual and organizational names have been changed to protect the privacy of those involved.

Working as a management consultant for the past several years, I have observed it is possible to "learn" but not apply. Therefore, personal application projects are given in an effort to make it easier to transfer principle into practice.

My sincere prayer is that you—and your organization or business—will become more effective and productive as a result of reading this book. I pray, too, that your example as a leader will stimulate many non-Christian leaders and businesspeople to turn to God's Word for direction in their own day-to-day leadership situations.

Myron D. Rush

FOREWORD

The work of the manager has seldom been more difficult than it is today. Low productivity, economic uncertainty, political instability, social unrest—these are just some of the forces that thrust new problems and challenges at the manager at a breathtaking rate. In response, management books and seminars are proliferating, and all promise solutions to the problems of the modern manager. Yet, these problems persist.

In *Management: A Biblical Approach*, Myron Rush brings us a refreshing and most helpful approach. Drawing timeless principles from the pages of the Bible, Myron presents a lively and practical guide for the manager who aspires to greater effectiveness and productivity. He provides the reader with a broad perspective of the task of managing, all the while giving careful attention to the needs of people, the organization's most basic resource. Each chapter concludes with practical applications designed to help integrate principles into daily practice.

I commend this book to all who are seeking to be more effective in guiding their organizations to success. Myron's years of experience as a manager and consultant, his obvious concern for people, and his commitment to biblical truth make this book a significant contribution to the art of management.

Lorne C. Sanny
Former President, The Navigators

CHAPTER 1

A BIBLICAL PHILOSOPHY OF MANAGEMENT

Recently I found myself sitting next to the senior pastor of a large California church on a flight from Los Angeles to Denver. When he learned I was a management consultant, he began sharing some of the management-related problems he was facing.

"Pastoring a growing church can be very frustrating," he said as we flew over Las Vegas, Nevada. "In our denomination, the pastor is constantly under pressure to produce growth in numbers and to develop new programs. However, if the church does grow, the pastor frequently becomes frustrated and feels incompetent to lead. Most pastors have not been trained to manage a large, dynamic organization."

As we crossed the Continental Divide and began our descent to Denver's Stapleton International Airport, he concluded, "Unfortunately, while most pastors feel capable of providing spiritual leadership, not many of us feel adequately prepared to manage an organization."

During the past several years I have heard similar statements from numerous pastors and Christian leaders. As in many other types of organizations, most managers and leaders in Christian organizations came up through the ranks. But unlike people in other profes-

1

sions, the Christian organization's management team probably attended a seminary or Bible college, where the educational program emphasized such subjects as homiletics, ecclesiology, eschatology, exegesis, soteriology, hermeneutics, Greek, and Hebrew.

All of these studies are certainly beneficial in helping an individual teach correct doctrine. But not one of them is designed to prepare a person to manage or lead an organization or group. Clearly, Christian organizations must begin giving more attention to management and leadership training because without effective management, no organization can carry on its most productive ministry.

Needed: A Biblical Approach to Management

The need for well-trained, highly qualified leaders in Christian organizations is emerging as a frequent topic of discussion throughout the Christian community. Many pastors, Bible college and seminary professors, and leaders and managers in parachurch organizations agree that we need better-prepared people to manage effectively the organizations God has raised up to accomplish His work.

Historically, most of Christendom has received its management philosophy and principles from the secular business world. Unfortunately, the secular management philosophy is often humanistic and materialistic. Authority and power are seen as a means of manipulating, using, and controlling people.

Most management textbooks, university professors, and management trainers and consultants define management as getting work done through others. This is the popular approach. Such a concept is very appealing to man's sinful nature because it gives managers and leaders the "right" to control and exploit those under them.

It is tragic that so many Christian organizations have accepted the world's philosophy of management. They are attempting to accomplish God's work using a management philosophy diametrically opposed to biblical principles. Consider, for example, the following passage:

> Then the mother of James and John, the sons of Zebedee, brought them to Jesus and respectfully asked a favor.
>
> "What is your request?" He asked.
>
> She replied, "In Your Kingdom, will You let my two sons sit on two thrones next to Yours?"
>
> But Jesus told her, "You don't know what you are asking!" Then He turned to James and John and asked them, "Are you able to drink from the terrible cup I am about to drink from?"
>
> "Yes," they replied, "we are able!"
>
> "You shall indeed drink from it," He told them. "But I have no right to say who will sit on the thrones next to Mine. Those places are reserved for the persons My Father selects."
>
> The other ten disciples were indignant when they heard what James and John had asked for.
>
> But Jesus called them together and said, "Among the heathen, kings are tyrants and each minor official lords it over those beneath him. But among you it is quite different. Anyone wanting to be a leader among you must be your servant. And if you want to be right at the top, you must serve like a slave. Your attitude must be like My own, for I, the Messiah, did not come to be served, but to serve, and to give My life as a ransom for many" (Matt. 20:20-28, TLB).

This passage describes the marked contrast between the world's philosophy of management and that of Jesus Christ. Leaders in a secular system of management often use their authority and power to "lord it over" the people under them, though the most enlightened ones certainly do not. In any case, Jesus said that the Christian should not behave that way.

The Christian leader is to serve those under him by helping them to reach maximum effectiveness. And the higher up in an organization a person goes, the more he is to serve. In fact, the head of the organization is to be totally at the service of those under him (like a slave is to a master).

The Bible provides an excellent case study of a leader. King Rehoboam chose to ignore God's approach to management and tried to "lord it over" his people. Rehoboam asked the elder statesmen of the nation how he should lead the people. They replied, "If today you will be a servant to these people and serve them and give them a favorable answer, they will always be your servants" (1 Kings 12:7). But King Rehoboam ignored their godly advice and used his power and authority to manipulate, control, and exploit the people. As a result, the nation rebelled against him and he lost the majority of his people.

The authoritarian approach to management stimulates discontent, frustration, and negative attitudes toward leadership. For the past several years, Management Training Systems, of which I am president, has been conducting research to determine what impact management philosophy has on productivity. Several hundred employees from both secular and Christian organizations have been asked the following question:

Assuming that the definition of management is *getting work done through others*, what does that definition communicate to you, the employee, concerning management's attitude toward its employees?

The responses most frequently stated were:

"Management sees people as tools to use to get a job done."

"The boss is interested in my back, not my brain."

"I'm paid to work, not think."

"I do the work, but the manager gets the credit."

"They are not interested in me as a person, only in what I can do for them."

"Management thinks it should make all of the decisions and my job is to carry them out."

Jesus knew that the world's approach to management and leadership creates relationship problems and poor productivity. He told the disciples not to pattern their lives after the world's philosophy, not to use authority and power to control people and pressure them to produce. He emphasized that the leader should use his authority and power to serve those under him. Therefore, the biblical approach to management can be defined as follows: *Management is meeting the needs of people as they work at accomplishing their jobs.*

As the manager gives himself to serving the needs of those under him, he will make a happy discovery. People will voluntarily, eagerly, and continually meet his needs in return. (See 1 Kings 12:7).

Do you want a clear description of what the Christian leader's attitude should be? Read Philippians 2:5-7: "Your attitude should be the kind that was shown us by Jesus Christ, Who, though He was God, did not demand and cling to His rights as God, but laid aside His mighty power and glory, taking the disguise of a slave and becoming like men" (TLB).

Lee Brase, a Christian leader on the West Coast, once told me, "Those of us in leadership positions frequently have difficulty with the idea of serving others. We tend to assume that since we have worked our way to the top, we are the ones who should be served. I guess we get to thinking we've earned that right."

He went on to explain that for the past fifteen years he had been training people to assume leadership positions. "I have discovered that if you *train* a man, he will become what you are," he said. "But if you serve him, the sky is the limit as to what he can become." He smiled and continued, "When I learned this, it freed me to serve men who have greater capacity than I have."

If the Christian enterprise is to accomplish the tasks for which God has raised it up, its leadership must apply the principles of management outlined in God's Word instead of those promoted and practiced by the secular world. That means we must direct our attention to God's Word for answers concerning how His work is to be managed.

Key Ingredients of a Successful Organization

Every management consultant and business administration professor has his own theory of what it takes to develop a successful organization. Most managers think they too "have a pretty good handle" on what their organizations need to succeed.

One top-level manager in an international parachurch organization said, "We must reorganize our operation if we expect to be successful as we continue to place staff in more and more countries around the world."

Another manager in the same organization told me, "We should broaden our ministry if we expect to be successful in the years ahead."

A pastor friend of mine said, "Our church needs a new facility if we are to be successful in reaching more people in the community."

An owner of a Christian bookstore recently told me, "My business would be a lot better if my store were in a different location."

The president of a Midwestern Christian college said, "We must expand our financial base if we expect to continue to grow."

Each of the needs mentioned above may be very important to the organization involved. However, none of them represents the key ingredients of a successful organization. The Bible identifies these ingredients in one of the most famous organizational case studies ever written. Containing only 195 words in the *New International Version*, this account offers invaluable data on the ingredients needed to develop and maintain a successful organization.

> Now the whole world had one language and a common speech. As men moved eastward, they found a plain in Shinar and settled there.
>
> They said to each other, "Come, let's make bricks and bake them thoroughly." They used brick instead of stone, and tar instead of mortar. Then they said, "Come, let us build ourselves a city, with a tower that reaches to the heavens, so that we may make a name for ourselves and not be scattered over the face of the whole earth."
>
> But the Lord came down to see the city and the tower that the men were building. The Lord said, "If as one people speaking the same language they have begun to do this, then nothing they plan to do will be impossible for them. Come, let Us go down and confuse their language so they will not understand each other."
>
> So the Lord scattered them from there over all the earth, and they stopped building the city. That is why it was called Babel—because there the Lord confused the language of the whole world. From there the Lord scattered them over the face of the whole earth (Gen. 11:1-9).

The account of building the Tower of Babel yields four key ingredients needed to develop a successful organization:

- Commitment to work on a goal (vv. 3-4)

- Unity among the people (v. 6)

- An effective communication system (vv. 1, 6)

- Doing the will of God (vv. 7-9 show they were *not*)

Every organization possessing these four ingredients will be successful.

Unlimited power is generated in an organization when people have a commitment to work on a goal, are united behind that commitment, and maintain effective communication. "If as one people speaking the same language they have begun to do this, then *nothing they plan to do will be impossible for them*" (v. 6).

Notice God says that when people are committed to work on a goal and have unity and a good communication system, nothing is impossible for them to achieve. Unless God stops them, they will accomplish whatever they set out to do. God knew the organization working on the Tower of Babel had the key ingredients for succes,s and if He didn't stop them, they would achieve their goal. Since they were not working on a goal that He approved, God stepped in and shut the project down.

How did He shut the project down? "Come, let Us go down and confuse their language" (v. 7). He disrupted their communication system. Once their communication broke down, their commitment to the project and their group unity were destroyed and the entire project failed. However, had they been working on a project God approved, they would surely have succeeded.

As a management consultant, I work with all types of organizations—both Christian and secular. Over the years I have observed that almost all organizational problems fall into three basic categories: lack of commitment on the part of the people to work on a clearly defined goal, lack of unity within and between departments or individuals, and poor communication. I have also observed that, in most cases, poor communication causes the other two problems.

The Objective of This Book

This book is designed to provide the principles of management outlined in the Bible. It also supplies the leadership and management tools needed to apply these biblical principles of management successfully. When God decided to accomplish His work through people, He knew they would need to organize in order to complete the tasks. Therefore, He made sure the Bible contained the management and organizational philosophies and principles needed to accomplish His work. These principles apply not only to Christian organizations, but to Christian leadership in any organization.

Chapter Summary

People involved in leading and managing God's work need to develop a biblical philosophy of management. There is an increasing awareness among Christian leaders that God's people need to become more effective in managing His work.

In the past the Christian community has failed to maintain a balance between "spiritual" and "organizational" leadership. Everyone recognizes the importance and necessity of spiritual leadership. However, only recently have Christian organizations begun to focus on the need for organizational and managerial leadership as well.

Currently most leaders in Christian organizations are receiving the bulk of their management training from the secular business community. This means many Christian leaders are attempting to manage God's work using a secular philosophy that has been condemned by God.

The world uses power and authority to "lord it over" people in an effort to get work done. The Bible teaches that authority is to be used to serve the needs of others. The Christian organization should adopt a biblical approach to management, an approach that focuses on meeting the needs of people under us as they work at accomplishing their jobs.

Four key ingredients that produce organizational success are commitment to work on a goal, unity among the people, an effective communication system, and a focus on doing God's will.

9

Personal Application

Make a list of your strengths and weaknesses as a leader or manager. As you study this book, keep track of the principles and tools needed to improve your management ability.

Study Matthew 20:20-28 and 1 Kings 12:1-20.

- In what ways have you possibly been lording it over those who work with or for you?

- What action can you take to correct this?

On two separate sheets of paper write the secular definition: "management is getting work done through others," and the biblical definition: "management is meeting the needs of others as they work at accomplishing their jobs." Ask various people you work with to describe what each definition of management communicates to them about what management thinks of them as employees.

Study Genesis 11:1-9. In which of the following areas do you feel your organization is the weakest?

- Commitment to work on a clearly defined goal.

- Unity among people within/between departments or groups.

- An effective communication system.

- A clear focus on the will of God.

CHAPTER 2

YOUR MOST VALUABLE RESOURCE

The personnel director of a mining company recently told me, "I have a frustrating job. When I hire new people, they are usually eager to go to work for us, but within a few weeks many of them are ready to quit."

As we discussed the reason for the rapid change in the employees' attitudes, he said, "I think part of the problem is that our employees feel management is more concerned about our expensive mining equipment than about our people."

An assistant pastor in our city invited me to lunch one day and during our conversation said, "Myron, I don't want to sound negative, but I'm about ready to leave the church where I'm supposedly assistant pastor."

I was shocked to hear this and asked, "What do you mean, 'supposedly assistant pastor?'"

"Well," he said, "I feel I have a lot more to offer than licking stamps, stacking chairs, and folding bulletins."

A few months later I received a letter from him postmarked from the West Coast, where he was working as director of admissions for a

Christian college. He wrote, "I miss the church, but at least here I feel needed and of value to someone."

People are an organization's most valuable resource. Yet in secular and Christian organizations alike, their value is frequently overlooked. Without people, an organization is nothing more than so many lines and boxes on a piece of paper called an organizational chart.

Irreducible Minimums of Management

Management activity may be reduced to two basic categories: the management of "things" and "ideas". These represent the irreducible minimums of management. Unfortunately, people often fall into the "things" category.

Generally it is easier to manage things than ideas because things are tangible while ideas are intangible. Things include budgets, facilities, equipment, and supplies. Things can be counted, placed on inventory, and in most cases, easily accounted for and controlled.

On the other hand, ideas can't be seen, are often difficult to evaluate, are sometimes hard to explain, can be easily ignored, and, in fact, frequently exist without management knowing about them. Therefore, most managers spend the bulk of their time managing things and frequently ignore the existence of ideas.

However, all things started out as an idea in someone's mind. Every man-made thing that exists—or has ever existed—was once an idea in the mind of a person. And the things of tomorrow are the ideas of today. Therefore, the leader or manager interested in progress—or in an organization's existence beyond the present—must make management of ideas his top priority. What an organization will be tomorrow depends on how well it manages people's ideas today.

Unfortunately, many managers view people in the organization basically as things to be used to get current work done. They fail to recognize that people are an organization's most valuable resource because many managers think of themselves as the only source of ideas. It is easy for managers to find themselves giving more attention to buildings, budgets, and equipment than to people, though people originated the ideas for these things.

The Unlimited Creativity of People

What is creativity and why is it important to an organization? Creativity can be defined as the making of something new, or the rearranging of something old. Using this definition, God and man are the only sources of creativity.

Not long ago a U.S.-based brain research center published a government-funded report stating that the creative capacity of the human mind is probably infinite. That should not come as a surprise. Approximately 4,000 years ago God said of people, "Nothing they plan to do will be impossible for them" (Gen. 11:16). God was announcing that man has the potential for unlimited creativity. What God said so long ago, science now supports—man has phenomenal creative ability.

When God was preparing to create man He said, "Let Us make man in Our image, in Our likeness" (Gen 1:26). Man was a very special creation because, of all God's creatures, he alone was given God's attribute of reason. Man is a rational being with decision-making power and creative ingenuity. This means man's mind is an organization's most valuable resource.

Letting Creativity Work for Your Organization

All people are creative. Everyone has the ability to make something new or rearrange something old. Creativity isn't a gift or talent possessed by a special few. One need not have artistic or musical talent to be creative.

People don't need special training to be creative. They don't have to exert special effort. Creativity is a natural product of man's thinking process. People will be as creative as an organization and its leadership will let them. Unfortunately, many organizations and managers fail to provide opportunities for their people to use their creativity. This is tragic, since tapping human creativity is the most effective means of increasing individual and organizational productivity.

Jesus illustrated the importance of increasing productivity by telling the Parable of the Talents. In this story the productive servants were rewarded and the unproductive person was severely punished.

The Parable of the Talents contains several biblical principles of management and leadership, two of which should be considered here. First, God expects the abilities and creativity of individuals to be utilized. Second, when an individual makes a contribution, he should be given recognition for his effort. Therefore, the Christian leader should encourage people in his or her group or organization to use their abilities and creativity in order to increase individual and organizational productivity. As this occurs, the leader must also give credit and recognition to those responsible for increasing production.

During World War II, Spartan Aircraft Company received a contract to manufacture a component of a fighter-bomber wing assembly. The company officials were told by the "experts" that it would take 18 months to gear up for production and 400 man-hours to produce each component. With a war on, this seemed like an eternity, so a meeting was called to discuss the problems with the entire workforce.

Spartan's management team asked the employees for their ideas on how to gear up for production sooner and how to reduce the man-hours required to manufacture each component. Using the ideas of their employees, the company was in full production in 8 months and using only 40 man-hours to make each part of the wing assembly.

Jim Anderson, the owner of Mile High Seed Company in Grand Junction, Colorado, called me one day and said, "I have a real problem. I am getting orders for 75 crates of garden seed per day, but we can only package and ship 35 crates. As a result, long back orders are causing me to lose over half of my potential business." Jim went on to explain that he had tried to solve the problem by automating part of the operation, but since he hadn't been in business long, the banks would not loan him the $500,000 needed to make the changes.

As we talked, I suggested he should go to the people working in the department and ask for their ideas for solving the problem. Jim didn't like the suggestion, stating that he felt it was his problem and his people shouldn't be bothered. But after some persuading on my part, he finally agreed to take the problem to the employees.

The next Friday at 3 P.M. Jim called a special meeting with the nine employees working in the flower and garden seed department and explained the situation to them. "If you have any ideas on how to solve the problem, I'm willing to listen," he said. The following Monday at 8 A.M., one of the department's employees walked into Jim's office with a diagram of their recommendations. Jim studied it a while and decided it might work.

Three months later Jim called me again. "Remember my problem with the flower and garden seed department? Well, I asked my employees if they had any ideas for solving the problem and they came up with a solution. We're now packaging and shipping 75 crates a day." He laughed and continued, "And it only cost $500 for a few materials."

The story doesn't end there. The following New Year's Eve, there was a knock on my door and in walked Jim and his wife. As we ate a few goodies and drank a cup of coffee, Jim grinned and said, "Let me fill you in on the latest development in our flower and garden seed department. We are now up to 105 crates a day, just using the ideas of the employees." Recently Jim came by my house and gave the latest figures: 145 crates a day.

Every Christian leader and manager should be concerned about making his organization as productive as possible. He should also keep in mind that God has given people unlimited creative ability for innovation and problem solving. Therefore, the leader should focus on putting people's creativity to work as a means of increasing productivity.

More Results of Using Creativity

Creativity finds solutions to organizational problems. When God said, "Nothing they plan to do will be impossible for them" (Gen. 11:6), that meant there is a solution to every organizational problem. Finding the solution results, in part, from soliciting and using proposals and ideas from people.

J. Paul Getty, at one time referred to as the wealthiest man in the world, made most of his fortune in the oil business. In the early years of his career, he owned a small piece of property 72-feet square in the Seal Beach oil field in California.

Oil derricks of the day were too large to fit on the small parcel of land, and before long Getty was being laughed at by fellow businessmen who referred to his small plot as "Getty's turnip patch." It was believed to be a worthless chunk of ground in the middle of the rich oil field.

However, Getty was determined to find a way to drill a well on it, knowing he would be sure to strike oil. One day he met with his drilling crew and described the situation to them, stating that if they had any ideas, he was open to their suggestions. Before long the employees came up with the idea of building a miniature oil derrick to fit on the miniature "turnip patch." They soon discovered, however, that there was only a 4-foot wide right-of-way from the road to the small site, making it seem impossible to move in equipment.

They wouldn't give up, and after a while, someone came up with the idea of building a miniature railroad track along the 4-foot wide right-of-way to carry their miniature derrick to their 72-foot square plot of ground. The idea was put into action, and before long, they had drilled a well that produced thousands of barrels of oil over a period of years.

During his lifetime, Getty proved time and again that organizational problems can be solved if leaders are willing to solicit creative ideas from people and then put them into practice.

Creativity finds new and better ways of accomplishing a task. Creativity stimulates progress and improvement. Any activity, program, or task can be improved using the creative ideas of people.

Steve Foster, the Sunday School superintendent of a growing church, had spent several months trying to figure out why the adult department in the Sunday School was not growing while all other departments were. Over a two-year period the church had almost doubled in size; however, many of the adults came only for the worship service.

Steve tried everything his years of Sunday School experience had taught him. He changed age groupings, ordered different material, changed the location of classes, and even changed teachers—all without much success.

Finally Steve decided to take the problem to the adults. He and the adult teachers planned a potluck dinner and invited the adults to come for an evening meal and planning session to improve their classes. During the meeting someone suggested people should be allowed to choose the class they wanted to attend rather than be assigned to classes by age groups. Another person suggested that topics change more frequently. Someone else shared ideas for new topics of study.

As a result of suggestions, the entire adult Sunday School program was changed to an elective system. Periodically a series of new topics would be offered, and individuals could choose their classes based on interest and need. Within a few months, the adult classes had grown so much they were looking for more classrooms and teachers.

Steve Foster's willingness to use the creative ideas of people allowed him to find new and improved ways to organize an adult Sunday School program. He later told me, "That experience taught me that my job as a leader is to identify the needs of those I'm supposed to be leading and then tap their ideas on how those needs can best be met."

The foreman of a mining company, Robert Stiles, supervised a crew responsible for constructing bulkheads in a mine. The five previous bulkheads had each taken five weeks to build; therefore, Stiles planned to schedule five weeks for the construction of the next one.

During a planning meeting, Stiles' boss, George Fox, explained the entire project was running behind schedule and asked Stiles if there was any way to shorten the construction time for the bulkheads. "Maybe, if I can get more men and equipment," Stiles replied with a certain amount of skepticism.

Since there wasn't enough money in the budget to hire more men or buy more equipment, both men concluded they would probably have to live with the five-week construction schedule. However, Stiles decided to ask his people for their ideas on how to shorten the schedule. To his surprise, they developed a plan that reduced construction time to two weeks instead of five—without adding people or equipment.

Both Foster and Stiles made an important discovery: by using the creativity of people, performance of a task or project can always be improved. Therefore, the leader or manager should always provide opportunities for people to use their creativity to improve the current functions, activities, programs, and projects of their organization.

Creativity costs nothing. It is there to be used. However, the costs of not using it can be astronomical. By using creativity the adults in Steve Foster's church developed a meaningful, growing adult Sunday School program. Robert Stiles reduced the time it took to build a bulkhead in a mine. Spartan Aircraft Company reduced the time it took to start production and build a component of an airplane wing assembly. Jim Anderson's people increased their ability to package and ship garden seed from 35 to 145 crates per day. All of this was done without hiring more people, purchasing expensive equipment, or increasing the size of the organization's budget.

Someone once said of creativity, "If you don't use it, you lose it." And the loss will be very costly in terms of productivity. Leaders who fail to use the creativity of their people, in most cases, eventually lose the people also.

People Need to Be Needed

Recently I was asked to conduct a seminar on biblical principles of management for a church in the Midwest. During an evening session coffee break, a lady in her mid-twentys approached me and asked, "Do you know about what time the session will end this evening?"

I said it would be over about 9 P.M. "Good," she remarked, "I live about twenty miles from here in another town and I don't want to be late getting home because I'm driving by myself."

As we talked I learned she was single, a high school teacher, and a member of the church. I knew the town she lived in had several good churches, so I asked why she chose to drive so far to church. "Well," she said, a little embarrassed, "I live about a mile from the First _____ Church, and I used to attend there regularly, but they don't seem to need Sunday School teachers, so I came here because they really needed help."

As she walked away I thought, *I have never seen a church that didn't need workers, especially Sunday School teachers*, but many churches do a poor job of communicating the need.

People need to be needed. They are innovative individuals full of ideas and solutions to problems, and they want to contribute. Much of an individual's sense of self-worth comes from contributing to the needs of his group or organization.

Unfortunately, many leaders and managers fail to recognize and use the unlimited potential of their human resources. Instead, they often find themselves overworked and frustrated with the increasing problems and responsibilities associated with operating an organization *for* people instead of *with* them. A good leader not only realizes people need to be needed, he makes sure all of those in his group or organization have an opportunity to use their skills, abilities, and creativity.

Jesus Christ knew this principle well. He came to give His life to and for people. That was His major goal. And He spent a great deal of time challenging and training people to get involved in "a piece of the action." For example, He said to Simon Peter and his brother Andrew, "Come, follow Me, and I will make you fishers of men" (Matt. 4:19).

The disciples recognized the value, importance, and potential of the job Jesus was offering them. They realized here was a Leader willing to use their abilities and creativity to do the same job He was doing. Their reaction to this type of offer is recorded in the next verse: "At once they left their nets and followed Him" (v. 20).

However, many leaders tell their people, "Follow me and you can have all of the jobs I don't want." Jesus not only recognized the unlimited potential and value of human creativity, He offered His followers training and opportunity to put their ability to work in a worthwhile cause. This is the mark of an excellent leader and manager of human resources.

An Organization's Greatest Barrier to Using Creativity

Even though creativity is an organization's most valuable resource, many leaders and managers fail to use it effectively. There is one major reason for this.

Organizational tradition limits the use of creativity. An organization travels through a life cycle much like that of a person. All man-made organizations are born, go through infancy, reach maturity, enter old age, and eventually die.

At birth and during infancy, an organization has not yet developed traditions. During this exciting stage of organizational development, people are encouraged to be as innovative and creative as possible. The general attitude is, "Try it—it just might work."

As a result, the organization develops a history of success and failures. The leaders and managers latch on to the things that work and use them over and over, while they avoid the methods that failed. Slowly, the things that work become tradition and a part of the organization's policies, procedures, methodology, and rules. This marks the beginning of the maturing process for the organization.

As more things consistently work, more traditions are established. Unfortunately, as more traditions develop, the organization and its leaders resist innovation and change. Tradition in itself is not bad. It becomes bad—and dangerous for the organization—only when it is allowed to stifle innovation and creativity. Tradition can and should play an important part in an organization, and it will as long as people are open to improving the traditional methods.

In its infancy an organization seeks to develop good, workable methods for accomplishing its goal. Ironically, as time goes by, there is a tendency for the method to become the goal. Thus, during the maturing process, the original mission, goal, or objective of an organization is slowly replaced by a new goal—maintaining the traditions of the method. This hastens the organization's aging process.

During the "old age" cycle of organizational life, virtually all innovation and creativity ceases. The organization rests comfortably on its past record of success, and all organizational energy is spent maintaining and protecting traditions. After all, they were responsible for the organization's achievement.

New ideas are quickly killed by statements such as:

- We have never done it that way before.

- Don't rock the boat.

- That will never work.

- Why risk failure and jeopardize our good standing and name when we know this works?

At this point the organization begins dying for lack of new ideas and vitality. Creativity is the life of an organization. When traditions stifle and kill it, the whole organization begins decaying.

Unfortunately, many organizations have died, but no one has noticed. An organization can die but the buildings are still there, the phone still rings, and someone is always there to answer it. However, that spark of life—innovation and creativity—that produced the organization's success has long since died. The only things remaining are the structures that house once-meaningful traditions that failed to keep pace with people's changing needs.

Therefore, every leader and manager should examine his or her traditions and make sure people are being encouraged to develop new and improved ways of accomplishing the organization's tasks, programs, and goals.

Chapter Summary

People are an organization's most valuable but least used resource. An organization is nothing more than boxes and lines on a piece of paper if its human resources are left untapped.

All management activities can be reduced to two basic functions—the management of "things" and "ideas." These are called the irreducible minimums of management. Most managers focus on things rather than ideas. However, all things begin as ideas. Therefore, the leader interested in progress should focus on managing ideas.

Man has almost unlimited creative potential. Creativity can be defined as the making of something new or the rearranging of something old. Being innovative and creative is a natural product of man's thinking process.

The organization that focuses on using the creativity of its people will discover workable solutions to its problems. It will find new and better ways of accomplishing its tasks. The organization's productivity will be increased as a result.

People need an opportunity to use their creativity, and if given a chance to be innovative, will offer their skills and abilities willingly. Unfortunately, an organization's traditions hinder the effective use of creativity. The leader and manager should keep in mind that creativity is unlike most organizational resources—if one doesn't use it, he loses it. Leaders who fail to use the creativity of their people eventually lose those people.

Personal Application

Examine your leadership and management activities to determine if you have been placing a greater emphasis on managing things or ideas.

Make a list of current organizational problems, and arrange to involve people in working on solutions to them.

Have your people suggest better ways of accomplishing certain tasks, and put these suggestions to work.

Ask people to identify organizational traditions currently hindering the use of creativity. Work with your people in determining what should be done to solve this problem.

Study Matthew 25:14-30 and see how many leadership and management principles you can identify.

CHAPTER 3

A PRODUCTIVE WORK ENVIRONMENT

An executive once told me, "It frustrates me to send people to management seminars. Most of them come back talking about what they learned, but they never seem to put it into practice."

In James 1:22 we read, "Do not merely listen to the Word, and so deceive yourselves. Do what it says." There is little if any value in developing a biblical philosophy of management unless the philosophy translates into action. To know and not apply is worse than not knowing.

It is possible to recognize that people have unlimited creative capacity and are an organization's most valuable resource, but still not know how to put those resources to work. This chapter focuses on the type of work environment a leader or manager must create in order to tap the unlimited creative potential of people.

The Leader or Manager Creates the Work Environment

For years, industrial psychologists, social scientists, and most management consultants and teachers have been aware of the influence the work environment has on individual productivity. As a result, some of the nation's largest industries are currently in the process of hiring "productivity managers" responsible for insuring that managers and supervisors focus on creating a work environment that stimulates productivity.

The leader is responsible for his group's work environment. Conditions within that environment are determined by the leader's

- Response to the group's needs

- Attitude toward people and work

- Use of authority

- Response to mistakes and failures

- Willingness to give the team proper credit for its accomplishments

The manager or leader interested in applying a biblical philosophy of management and tapping the unlimited creative potential of people must:

- Create a trust relationship between himself and his group

- Give decision-making power to all individuals within the group

- Turn failures and mistakes into positive learning experiences for the group

- Constantly give proper recognition to the group and its individuals for accomplishments

All of these elements interlock and must be applied consistently in order to develop and maintain a productive work environment. For example, there is little value in a leader trying to demonstrate he trusts his people if he is unwilling to let them make decisions. Similarly, the manager who tries to give decision-making power to people but is unwilling to work at turning failures and mistakes into positive learning experiences will discover his people are reluctant to make decisions.

Develop a Trust Relationship

Trust is the most important element in the development and maintenance of a productive work environment. Trust stimulates security and confidence, two prerequisites to innovation and creativity. On the other hand, mistrust produces frustration, insecurity, and fear—all major deterrents to creative thinking and innovative action.

Mary Turner, a friend of our family, is office manager for a missions organization. She called one evening and asked, "What do you do when your boss says you can do something and then doesn't let you?" Before I could respond, she continued, "I'm getting fed up with this job. Last week my boss said I could hire another girl for the office. I interviewed several people and yesterday offered a girl the job. Today my boss changed his mind. He said I couldn't hire anyone and didn't even give me a reason."

The longer she talked, the more upset she became. "And guess who has to call the girl and tell her she doesn't have a job?" she said angrily. "That's right. I do."

After discussing her boss for a while, Mary concluded, "I'll tell you one thing. From now on I'll get things in writing from him before I do anything. You just can't trust a person like that."

Mary's mistrust of her boss led to frustration, low morale, loss of productivity, and eventual termination. A few weeks later she came through town on her way to a new job. "I hated to leave the organization," she said. "But it got to the point where I wasn't doing justice to the job or myself. You just can't do your best working for a boss you can't depend on."

Trust begins with the leader or manager. Last summer I spent a weekend at a boys ranch in the Rocky Mountains. All of the boys there had been in trouble with the law. Some had stolen money, cars, or merchandise.

During my stay the owner said, "I've been in this work for over thiry years, and I've discovered that in most cases these boys are trust-worthy if you demonstrate you really trust them first." He concluded, "The trouble is, most people don't trust these kids, so they feel they might as well go ahead and steal or get in trouble—they'll be blamed for it, anyway."

As I listened to this wise man, I was reminded of a manager at a seminar I had conducted. His name was Paul Evans. During the day, we discussed the importance of trust. After the session Paul came to me and said, "You don't know my people. I have an employee I don't dare trust—and she knows it, too!"

He shook his head and continued. "Every time I'm gone for the day, she takes three or four coffee breaks, leaves early for lunch and returns late, and doesn't get half her work done." He frowned and said, "I'm about ready to fire her."

I was scheduled to return for another training session in six weeks so I said, "I'll make a deal with you. If you'll honestly demon-strate to this employee that you trust her and she fails to show any improvement, during the next session I'll retract what I said today about the value of trust."

He smiled like the cat that had just swallowed the canary and said, "You've got yourself a deal."

I must admit that six weeks later as I drove into the company's parking lot, I was wondering if I would have to retract what I had said about the value of trust. However, Paul met me before the session started and said with a smile, "You know, I really can't believe what is happening with that girl."

He explained she was the only employee in the office with a mas-ter's degree in accounting, so he had asked her to teach a short accounting course for some of the new workers. It had been planned as a three-week course for three other employees. However, some of the other managers heard about it and they ended up with twelve workers and a course lengthened to six weeks.

"I have to admit there has been a big improvement in her attitude," he said. "For example, just this week she stayed late two nights in a row to catch up on some extra work, and she never complained once."

Every leader and manager should learn what the owner of the boys ranch and Paul Evans discovered. Trust begins with the leader. He or she must be willing to demonstrate trust if people are to be trustworthy.

Trust builds confidence and stimulates production. A work environment based on trust gives employees the confidence and security needed to use their creativity. You see, innovation involves risk. The person who feels he can't trust his leaders will never take the risks required to develop new and better ways of accomplishing a task. Trust produces innovation, but mistrust breeds stagnation.

One morning, Carl Williams, the division manager of a wholesale firm, invited me to breakfast. Halfway through the bacon and eggs, he said, "I wanted to talk with you because I'm afraid I'm about to be fired from my job." I was shocked because I had recently conducted a management training program for Carl and several of his supervisors and had been impressed with his managerial insights and abilities.

"What's the problem?" I asked.

"Well," he began, "this past year I failed to keep my inventory under control. As a result, my division ended the year several hundred thousand dollars in the red." He was obviously upset and took a deep breath as he concluded. "I received a call from the president yesterday saying he wants to talk with me. I'm flying back to our corporate office tomorrow to meet with him—I assume to be fired."

I offered Carl what few encouraging words I could and told him I would call him if I heard of any jobs he might want.

Three days later Carl called and said, "I thought I should let you know I don't need another job. The president wanted to meet me personally to assure me he still had confidence in my ability to manage the division. He thought I probably needed some encouragement as a result of the bad year I had just experienced." Carl ended the conversation by saying, "One thing is certain. I don't intend to let my boss down. If he thinks I can do the job, I'll prove he's right."

The next year Carl's division earned the largest profit in the entire corporation. I have had several conversations with Carl since that incident. More than once he has indicated that knowing his boss trusts him has given him the confidence and motivation needed to develop a highly productive group of employees.

By contrast, I think of another experience. I was conducting an organizational analysis for a Christian school when one of the custodians, Jack Peterson, told me, "You'll find morale and productivity pretty low around here."

"Why's that?" I asked.

"Since we got our new boss, people seem to get fired without much notice or reason," he said. "I've been here nine years, but I'm looking for another job. I keep thinking, *Who knows, I may be next.*"

For Carl Williams, knowing his boss trusted him gave him the self-confidence and determination he needed to improve his division's productivity greatly. On the other hand, not being able to trust his boss caused Jack Peterson to start looking for another job. These are classic examples of the impact trust has on an individual's self-confidence and personal productivity.

Give Decision-Making Power to People

Giving decision-making power is the second step in developing a productive work environment. From antiquity people have been forming organizations. However, none has withstood the test of time. All man-made organizations eventually become extinct. Often their demise is due to their inability to remain flexible enough to meet the needs of a changing society. In other words, the organization fails to create an ongoing work environment that continually encourages people to use their creativity and innovative ideas to meet ever-changing needs—both within the organization and among those it serves.

Jesus Christ is the best manager and developer of human resources the world has ever seen. He created a work environment for those He trained that allowed them to start the church, and it has continued through 2,000 years of man's most rapidly changing industrial, political, and social environments. Therefore, the manager or leader interested in creating an effective and productive work environment should pattern it after the principles used by Christ.

Two of the most important of the principles are: demonstrate trust, and give decision-making power. Turning one's decision-making power over to another person is itself the ultimate expression of trust. However, it not only demonstrates trust, but also provides the greatest possible opportunity for people to use their creativity.

Decision-making power provides freedom to apply one's creativity and innovative ideas. Decision-making power can be defined as the right to determine what action will be taken. Jesus said to His disciples, "Go into all the world and preach the Good News to all creation" (Mark 16:15). Here Jesus stated the goal, but He gave the disciples decision-making power concerning how the goal was to be accomplished. As a result, they used their creativity and ingenuity to formulate plans for accomplishing the goal.

The result of Jesus giving His followers freedom to decide how to reach people with the Gospel is seen a few years later, when Paul and Silas are described as men who "have turned the world upside down" (Act 17:6, KJV).

Decision-making power paves the way for an organization or group of people to be more responsive to people's needs, both within and outside the group. It allows for flexibility and change, and is the most effective way of tapping an individual's unlimited creative potential and channeling it toward the achievement of a specific goal.

Turn Failures into Positive Learning Experiences

Fear of failure is one major reason why managers and leaders are reluctant to give decision-making power to other individuals. However, the person concerned about creating a productive work environment for a group must accept a certain amount of failure. He must also learn to turn that failure into a positive learning experience for all concerned.

Fear of failure stifles creativity and reduces productivity. Fear is one of man's worst enemies, stifling innovation and destroying productivity. In Jesus' Parable of the Talents, the servant receiving one talent said, "Master ... I knew that you are a hard man, harvesting where you have not sown, and gathering where you have not scattered seed. So I was afraid and went out and hid your talent in the ground" (Matt. 25:24-25). The servant's fear caused him to do nothing with the talent he had been given, and as a result he produced nothing.

Lawrence Appley, former president of the American Management Association, understood the devastating effect fear of failure has on people. In a speech on the subject, he said:

> Besides, what is so terrible about making a mistake? It is from our mistakes that we learn. Without mistakes there can be no progress. It is hard to realize why almost paralyzing fear of error curbs the initiative of so many men in management. This fear of error is one of the main reasons for costly red tape and controls that are established to insure

against errors which, if made, could not cost anywhere near as much as the controls do. It is this intolerance of mistakes that curbs decentralization of responsibility and authority. It is unreasonableness of this kind that causes able men to keep their noses clean and their mouths shut.

Fear of failure reduces the willingness to risk. Risk can be defined as exposing oneself to the possibility of loss or harm. Many leaders and managers fear change, innovation, and creative ideas because of the risk involved. There is always the possibility the creative idea might fail and the group or organization might experience loss or harm. This fear presents a constant temptation to settle for what has been tried and proven in the past.

The Parable of the Talents provides a vivid example of the role *willingness to risk* plays in productivity and success. Two of the servants risked failure in order to succeed. Ironically, the one servant unwilling to risk possible failure failed precisely because he was not willing to risk.

During the early years of J. C. Penney's career, he worked as a salesclerk in a department store. On several occasions, his supervisor mentioned he hoped to own his own store someday. Some twenty-five years later, after starting the J. C. Penney Company, Penney returned to the store where he had received much of his training and was surprised to see his former supervisor still working there. When Penney asked him why he had never bought a store of his own, he said, "Oh, too much risk. Here I have a decent job with good security, but if I owned my own store, I might go broke."

Many leaders promote that type of work environment by their attitude toward risk and failure. The manager wishing to develop a highly productive work environment must promote innovation and change and be willing to live with the risk involved. In order to achieve their full potential, people must be permitted to make mistakes, or even to fail.

During my junior college days, I played basketball for Central College in McPherson, Kansas. At halftime during a regional tournament, our coach chewed us out royally for missing so many shots the first half. As he lectured us in the locker room, he said, "The next person to miss a shot is going to sit on the bench the rest of the game." He raised his voice and his face got red as he stopped in front of each of us, shook his finger in our faces, and asked, "Is that clear?"

It was perfectly clear, and all of us returned to the court the second half thinking, *I'm not going to be the first to shoot and miss.* As a result, none of us would shoot when we got the ball, and we quickly got further behind. Our coach realized his mistake, called time-out, and told us to forget what he had said in the locker room and get back out there and do our best. We finally won by two or three points.

Our fear of the consequences made us unwilling to risk a shot. Until that fear was removed, we fell further and further behind. However, as soon as our coach encouraged us to try, even if we missed, we were willing to shoot the ball.

I have never forgotten the lesson I learned that night regarding freedom to fail. Unfortunately, I have observed many leaders and managers who have not yet learned the importance of encouraging people to try even if it does mean making a mistake or failing.

Failures can become positive learning experiences. Anyone can criticize and condemn a person's failures, but effective leaders and managers work with people to turn their mistakes and failures into positive learning experiences. Any manager can discipline a subordinate for his shortcomings, but it takes considerable leadership skill to help a person recognize his error, learn from it, and still be motivated to try again.

When an individual or group makes a serious mistake or fails, the leader should:

1. Meet with those involved in the mistake and determine the cause.

2. Work with the individual or group to determine what should have been done to avoid the mistake and what needs to be done to correct it.

3. Let the person who failed do the project or activity again in order to make proper corrections.

When dealing with mistakes, the leader or manager should keep in mind that his job is to meet the work-related needs of those in his group or organization. Therefore, when a person has failed at a task, the leader should determine whether he contributed to the failure himself by not properly meeting individual needs.

In applying step one, the leader should ask those involved if any aspect of the failure was the result of work-related needs not being met. This demonstrates the leader's willingness to accept part of the blame and shows he wants to learn from the mistake. In most cases the manager or leader will discover he could have done some things to minimize the risk for the individual or group.

Step two provides opportunity for the leader to use the creativity of those involved to correct the problem and, at the same time, provide an excellent learning experience. However, many leaders try to work out the solution by themselves. This communicates to people that they are not trusted or capable of correcting the problem, and it undermines their self-confidence.

Step three is one of the most important aspects of turning failures into positive learning experiences. Here again, the leader may be tempted to correct the problem himself. Or he may want to assign the activity to someone else. Neither of these actions is acceptable. If the mistake or failure is to become a positive learning experience for those involved, they must not only have an opportunity to develop a solution but also to carry it out. Failure to provide such an opportunity communicates that the manager or leader no longer trusts those who failed. As a result, in the future they will be reluctant to take the risks sometimes necessary to develop and implement new and improved ways of accomplishing the task.

Jesus was a master at turning people's mistakes and failures into positive learning experiences using this three-step process. For example, the disciples revealed their lack of faith and spiritual maturity at the feeding of the 5,000 (Matt. 14:13-21); and the feeding of the 4,000 (Matt. 15:32-39); and when trying in vain to heal a young boy (Matt. 17:14-21). However, Jesus continued to assign His work to the disciples, telling them, "Go into all the world and preach the Good News to all creation" (Mark 16:15).

Even though the disciples failed repeatedly, Jesus continued to give them the task of ministering to people. He never told them, "Since you blew the last assignment, you're no longer qualified to be My disciples; I'll have to replace you with someone else." No. Jesus allowed His disciples to fail, to learn from the experience, and to try again. As a result, He produced people who, though they had once failed to heal a sick boy (Matt. 17:14-21), were later able to heal a lame beggar (Acts 3:1-10). And even though Peter once denied knowing Christ, he matured to the point where he was ready to die for Him (Acts 5:17-42).

J. C. Penney's first store was located near Denver, Colorado. The store was never successful, but Penney was determined—he would not give up, no matter what. He learned from his mistakes and opened another store in Wyoming. His second store was a success, and as everyone knows, he went on to build a national chain of dry goods stores. However, if Penney had given up following his first failure, he would never have achieved what he did.

Failure can be one of life's best teachers if people are given an opportunity to correct their mistakes and succeed. On the other hand, if handled improperly by the leader, failure can completely destroy an individual's self-image, motivation, and productivity. Failure can turn a courageous, insightful person into a fearful and defeated one.

Provide Proper Recognition

Throughout the Bible, God emphasizes the importance of giving recognition to those who deserve it. This principle is clearly demonstrated by Jesus in the Parable of the Talents. To each of the productive servants his master said, "Well done, good and faithful servant! You have been faithful with a few things; I will put you in charge of many things" (Matt. 25: 21, 23).

We are commanded, "Do not withhold good from those who deserve it, when it is in your power to act" (Prov. 3:27). Again, we read, "Give everyone what you owe him: If you owe taxes, pay taxes . . . if respect, then respect; if honor, then honor" (Rom. 13:7).

These passages express an important principle of leadership and management: Give credit and recognition to people for their accomplishments. Giving recognition costs nothing. Yet it is one of the most overlooked and least used tools of motivation a leader has at his disposal.

During an organizational analysis of a government agency, an employee said to me, "Just once I wish someone around here would tell me how I'm doing. I've worked here two years and I don't know if I'm doing a good or bad job." He went on to say, "Sometimes I'm not even sure they know I work here!"

As a management consultant I have heard that complaint hundreds of times in both Christian and secular organizations. Most leaders and managers acknowledge that giving recognition is important, but few take the time and effort required to do it.

Recognition demonstrates that you need and appreciate people's contributions. Not one leader in a million would say he or she does not appreciate the contributions of people. However, many communicate that by their failure to voice appreciation for their people's efforts.

I recently visited a church a friend of mine attends. During the morning service, two young women sang a beautiful song that obviously spoke to the hearts of many in the congregation. Afterward the pastor approached the pulpit and said, "I'd like to draw your attention to the announcements in the bulletin."

I turned to my friend and said, "He just missed an excellent opportunity to recognize the talent of those two young women and show appreciation for their willingness to use it in the church."

My friend looked at me and nodded. "That's right," he said, "and that's part of the reason we have problems getting people to volunteer for anything around here."

People need to feel needed. Giving recognition helps meet that need. By saying, "Well done, good and faithful servant! You have been faithful with a few things; I will put you in charge of many things" (Matt. 25:21), the master in the Parable of the Talents was communicating to his servants that he needed and appreciated their efforts and contributions. The leader or manager wanting to develop a productive work environment must continually do the same.

Recognition motivates people to volunteer their services. I once heard a director of Christian education say during a Sunday School convention, "If you need more Sunday School teachers, make heroes out of the ones you already have." It took me a while to see the wisdom in that statement. When people are recognized publicly for their contributions and achievements, others are more willing to work at the same job because they also can expect recognition.

I have never seen a leader or manager properly recognize his people in private and public and still lack help and assistance. Such leaders have a ready reserve of workers to assist in accomplishing the group's tasks. Giving recognition stimulates people to use their creativity to achieve the group's or organization's goals and objectives. However, the leader who ignores opportunities to provide proper recognition will have a difficult time getting people to use their skills, gifts, and abilities fully in achieving the group's goals.

Chapter Summary

The leader or manager is responsible for creating a positive work environment. People have unlimited potential to be creative and achieve greater levels of productivity. However, the work environment greatly influences how many of an individual's gifts, skills, and abilities are used.

To maintain a highly productive work environment, the leader must develop a trust relationship with his people, give them decision-making power that allows them to use their creativity, turn mistakes and failures into positive learning experiences, and provide proper recognition.

Trust begins with the leader or manager. Unless people feel they can trust the actions of management, they will be reluctant to take the risks sometimes needed to apply new and innovative ideas and improvements.

Decision-making is the right to determine what action will be taken. Giving decision-making power is one of the most effective means of communicating trust. It gives people freedom to apply their creativity in developing more productive methods of accomplishing a task.

As the leader or manager gives decision-making power to people, he must be prepared to help them turn mistakes and failures into positive learning experiences. Fear of failure hinders people from being willing to use their potential to increase the organization's productivity. Failures can be turned into positive learning experiences as the leader helps people identify the cause of the mistake, lets them determine what should be done to correct the problem, and finally, gives those who failed an opportunity to correct the mistake.

The leader must give people recognition they deserve because doing so shows the leader needs and appreciates their efforts and accomplishments. It also motivates people to volunteer their services to accomplish the task or goal.

The four elements of the productive work environment described in this chapter create an atmosphere in which people's unlimited potential can be put to work to accomplish the group's or organization's goals. The leader must keep in mind that all of these elements must be applied consistently in order to be effective.

Personal Application

Evaluate your relationship with each person in your team or work group. What could you be doing to improve the trust relationship with them?

Examine the type and level of decision-making power currently being given to people in your group or department. What will you do to give them more opportunity to use their creative potential?

Think of recent or current mistakes or failures within your group and how you handled them. What could have been done to make them more positive learning experiences?

Develop a plan for giving your people more private and public recognition. Keep track of the effect recognition has on the productivity of the group.

CHAPTER 4

THE TEAM SPIRIT

Chapter 2 pointed out the unlimited potential and creativity of the individual. Chapter 3 explained the type of work environment the leader or manager must create in order to tap that potential. This chapter explains how an individual's skills, gifts, and abilities can be better used and increase organizational productivity.

A team can be defined as two or more people moving along a path of interaction toward a common goal. Several key words in this definition indicate important principles of team dynamics. First, a team consists of "two or more people." Second, the group is "interacting" and communicating. Third, the team has "a common goal." Unless these three elements are present, a team does not exist.

Two or more people working on the same project, if they do not communicate, are not a team. People working together and communicating, whose efforts aren't focused on a common goal, are not a team. In order to have a team, two or more people must be communicating and working on the same goal. These important principles of team dynamics will be explored in detail in this chapter.

The Purpose of a Team

A team helps people accomplish more than they could working individually. Two people effectively working together as a team can accomplish much more than two individuals working alone. This principle is clearly expressed in Ecclesiastes 4:9-13.

> Two can accomplish more than twice as much as one, for the results can be much better. If one falls, the other pulls him up; but if a man falls when he is alone, he's in trouble.

> Also, on a cold night, two under the same blanket gain warmth from each other, but how can one be warm alone? And one standing alone can be attacked and defeated, but two can stand back-to-back and conquer; three is even better, for a triple-braided cord is not easily broken. (TLB).

As this passage suggests, both the quantity and quality of work improve when one becomes a part of an effective team.

Jesus Christ knew and applied this principle consistently. He formed a team of twelve men and trained them to carry on His work after His return to heaven. Mark 6:7-13 describes Jesus dividing His twelve-man team into six two-man teams and sending them out to preach the Gospel, heal the sick, and cast out demons. Why did Jesus send six two-man teams instead of twelve individuals? Because He understood the principle of team dynamics as recorded in Ecclesiastes 4:9—if individuals can learn to work as a team, they will be much more effective than working alone. Therefore, Jesus taught His disciples to work together as a team to accomplish a common goal.

A team allows people to use their gifts, skills, and talents more effectively. Everyone has strengths and weaknesses, and one's weaknesses tend to reduce the effectiveness of his strengths. For example, let's suppose that Bill, an excellent tax consultant who is very poor at meeting the public, starts his own tax-consulting business. Even though he is an expert on taxes, Bill's business probably will fail because of his inability to deal with clients and the general public.

In order to capitalize on his strengths and compensate for his weakness, Bill needs to team up with someone strong in meeting the public. Let' suppose he hires Betty, an outgoing, warm, and personable receptionist who knows nothing about the tax business but is excellent at handling clients and the general public. By working as a team, Bill and Betty will probably be able to develop a successful business because each will be able to work in his or her area of strength.

One purpose of a team, then, is to bring people together who can compensate for one another's weaknesses as they focus on using their own gifts, skills, and talents.

Jesus modeled the church on this team approach to Christian service. We read:

> Some of us have been given special ability as apostles; to others He has given the gift of being able to preach well; some have special ability in winning people to Christ, helping them to trust Him as their Savior; still others have a gift for caring for God's people as a shepherd does his sheep, leading and teaching them in the ways of God.

> Why is it that He gives us these special abilities to do certain things best? It is that God's people will be equipped to do better work for Him, building up the church, the body of Christ, to a position of strength and maturity (Eph. 4:11-12, TLB).

This passage points out that individuals have different gifts and strengths. These are to be used to assist one another as the team works at accomplishing the goal—in this case building up the church and bringing it to spiritual maturity.

God doesn't expect an individual to be strong in every area. Each person has been given his own unique set of gifts, skills, creative talents, and weaknesses. Unfortunately, many leaders and managers think their chief aim is to eliminate—or at least greatly reduce—people's areas of weakness. Figure 1 illustrates the fallacy of such thinking.

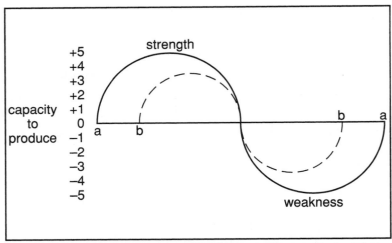

Figure 1. A person has both strengths and weaknesses, as illustrated by line "a". Line "b" shows that excessive work to reduce one's weaknesses also greatly reduces his strengths.

Line "a" in figure 1 represents a person's normal strengths and weaknesses. By expending a considerable amount of time, energy, and money in training, a leader can help a person greatly reduce his shortcomings. However, as the dotted line "b" shows, if excessive time and effort is spent trying to eliminate weaknesses, the strengths will be reduced as well due to lack of use. This does not mean a person should not try to reduce his weaknesses. But excessive concentration on one's shortcomings greatly reduces his capacity to produce.

Therefore, the leader interested in using people's gifts, skills, and creativity to increase productivity should allow them to work in their areas of strength. Since individuals also have weaknesses, the leader or manager should organize people into teams in which one person's strengths compensate for another's weakness, as illustrated in figure 2.

This approach to team building gives people greater job satisfaction, more opportunities to use their creativity, more motivation, and greater productivity. People are always happier and more productive when they can work at something they are good at and enjoy. This does not mean that people should ignore their shortcomings and turn down opportunities to develop new skills. Every person should seek to

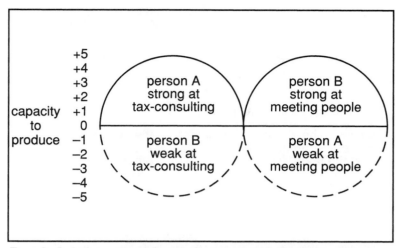

Figure 2. By letting one person's strengths compensate for another's weaknesses, a team can maintain a high level of productivity.

develop his skills and improve his abilities. However, leaders and managers should make sure people have the opportunity to work in their area of interest and strength as a means of increasing productivity and compensating for the weaknesses of others. If leaders spent more time making sure people were working in their areas of strengths and interests, and less time focusing on the weaknesses of the individual, they would discover everyone concerned would be happier and more productive—including themselves.

Needs That Members Bring to the Team

Each team member brings his own unique set of needs to the team. However, there are four critical needs that all team members have in common. Unless these are met, the individual will not become a productive part of the group. The leader should be aware of these needs and make sure he and the other team members are meeting them. These four key needs are shown in figure 3.

The need to use one's skills and gifts to assist the team's efforts. The age of computers and automation has introduced time-saving and

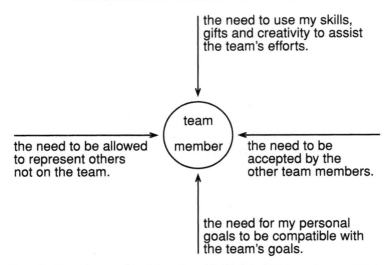

Figure 3. Every team member brings these four needs with him to the team. Unless these needs are met, the individual's contribution will be limited.

energy-saving electronic gadgets and machines. Unfortunately, it has also brought us a new problem—identity crisis.

Today computers, electronic equipment, and machines are able to do most of the tasks man has prided himself on doing in the past. Furthermore, in most cases, the machines can do the work faster and with fewer mistakes than people can. As a result, many people are asking, "Who am I? What is my role in life? Where do I fit in society?"

An industrial psychologist recently told me, "It is becoming increasingly important for managers and leaders to recognize the importance of letting people use their skills on meaningful projects." He went on to say, "Man's self-image is directly tied to his perception of the value and importance of his contribution to a meaningful job."

This being true, the leader wishing to develop and maintain an effective work group or team needs to make sure each team member has the opportunity to use his gifts and talents in making a meaningful contribution to the team's goals and objectives.

Lorraine was the most qualified member of the group of secretaries working in the principal's office of a large high school. She had experience as an executive secretary, office manager, and bookkeeper. She had also conducted several secretarial science workshops for those beginning their careers in secretarial work. However, since she was the newest "girl" on the job, she was given the tasks other secretaries didn't want—filing, sorting mail, and stuffing envelopes. As a result, her skills and abilities were not being used. She became frustrated with her job and resentful of the other women. She began losing her self-confidence. Less than six months after taking the job, she resigned.

Lorraine quit not because her job was too difficult, but because her abilities and talents were not being used.

The need to be accepted by the other team members. A person not only needs an opportunity to use his skills and abilities to assist the team's efforts, but he also needs fellow team members to accept him as part of the team. This is frequently a problem for new team members.

Kathy Walters was promoted from office manager to personnel director in a parachurch organization. Her new position made her a part of the president's planning team. Kathy had been a member of the team for four months when she cornered me during a coffee break at a management seminar.

"How can a person work with a team when the other team members treat you like you don't belong there?" she asked disgustedly. "For the past four months I've sat through weekly planning meetings feeling like my ideas and opinions really aren't wanted. I don't know if it's because I'm a woman or if I have bad breath, but if they don't want my help, I have plenty of work in my department to keep me busy."

If a person doesn't feel accepted by fellow team members, he is usually reluctant to contribute to the team's goals. Therefore, each team member should make sure he demonstrates acceptance of others on the team. That does not mean team members must always agree. However, it does mean they do not ignore the presence, ideas, and contributions of any members.

The need to pursue team goals compatible with personal goals. This is the most important need a member brings to his team. It will be difficult for an individual to make a long-term commitment to a team if his personal goals aren't compatible with the team's. Therefore, the leader or manager should make every effort to place people on the team who will receive personal satisfaction and fulfillment by helping the team achieve its goal and purpose.

If an individual's personal goals are compatible with the team's, he will be motivated to give his time, energy, and abilities to insure the team's goals are met. On the other hand, if an individual's goals are in conflict with the team's, he will be tempted to give attention to personal goals and ignore the group's.

When recruiting team members, many managers make the mistake of looking at an individual's skills and abilities without considering his personal goals. Having talent and ability needed by the group does not guarantee an individual could—or should—serve on the team.

Eric Robinson had several years' experience in both housing and commercial construction. Therefore, he seemed like an ideal person to be on his church's building and grounds committee, a group responsible for the maintenance and upkeep of the church's physical facilities. After being asked several times, Eric reluctantly agreed to serve.

However, Eric's interest was in constructing new buildings, not maintaining older ones. As a result, every time he was asked to help fix up the building, he complained that the church should be putting its money in a new building fund instead of wasting time and money repairing the old building. Both Eric and his fellow committee members became frustrated and Eric eventually resigned from the group.

In Eric's case the leaders failed to make sure his goals and interests were compatible with the team's. They only considered Eric's abilities. Eric had the ability needed, but his personal interests and goals conflicted with the committee's. As a result, both he and the group became frustrated.

The need to represent people and groups outside the team. Every team member brings a "political" dimension and need to the team. That is, each individual is consciously or subconsciously representing friends, peers, special interest groups, and value systems as he or she contributes to the team's goals.

For example, the board of directors of a certain parachurch organization contains, among others, a businessman, the head of a missions organization, and a seminary professor. During a recent policy-setting meeting, the businessman focused on how the policy would be interpreted by the business community and therefore impact fund-raising. The missions representative emphasized the new policy's impact on the Christian community overseas in various cultural settings. The seminary professor talked about the theological ramifications of the policy and how various religious groups would feel about it.

In order for an individual to feel he is making a meaningful contribution, the team's decisions and actions must reflect the thinking and values of individuals and groups he represents. If the businessman on the board feels the team's emphasis is not compatible with the concerns of the business community, he will feel he has personally failed.

Therefore, it would be improper for a leader to ask a person to serve on a team knowing that his special interest groups and value system could not properly be represented.

The Key to Building Productive Teams

People form organizations in order to accomplish projects and goals unattainable by one individual. The same principle applies within the organization. Organizations form teams to accomplish things that couldn't be done well by individuals. Therefore, developing and maintaining productive teams is an excellent way for an organization to increase its productivity without increasing its budget or capital investments.

The team goal or mission is the key to developing and maintaining a productive team. The leader or manager interested in developing a productive team should involve the team members in developing or refining the team goal. Such participation gives the team ownership of the goal and motivates commitment to its accomplishment. A team will work much harder to achieve a goal it helped design than one developed solely outside the team.

As figure 4 illustrates, a team member is either being drawn into the team and a closer working relationship with other team members, or he is being pulled away from it by conflicting issues and unmet needs.

If team members participate in developing or refining the goal, there is less risk of developing conflicting issues and unmet needs. On the other hand, if the team's goal is developed solely outside the team, in all probability one or more of the conflicting issues and needs will develop. Each additional issue reduces the individual's commitment to the team's goal.

Therefore, the manager or leader should strive to let the team help formulate their goal. In doing so, he will discover the team accomplishes more and develops and maintains a tension-free work environment.

Roles Team Members Play

Team dynamics play an important part in determining a team's success or failure. Each individual is continually playing a positive or negative role within the team. On the positive side are *production* and *maintenance* roles. The negative can best be defined as an anti-team role. Production roles focus on a task or job, maintenance roles focus on others in the team, and *anti-team* roles focus on self.

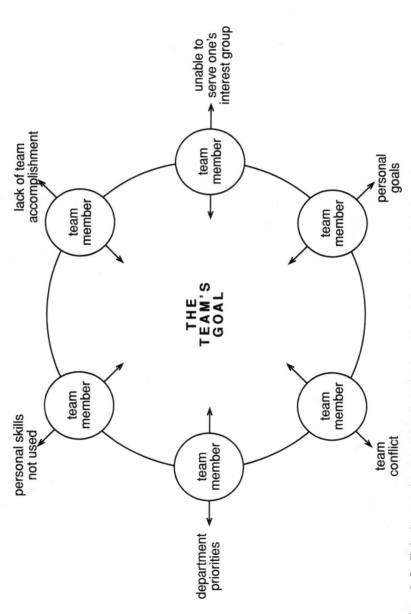

Figure 4. Conflicting issues and unmet needs pull members away from their commitment to the team. However, the team's goal or mission is the only thing that can pull a team together into a productive group.

Production roles focus on a task or job. A person contributing to team production generally plays one of the following roles:

ORGANIZER: Works with the group to identify, assign, and schedule tasks and activities.

INITIATOR: Offers suggestions and recommendations for the group's consideration.

DATA COLLECTOR: Gathers facts, figures, and other information needed to assist the group with its work.

FACILITATOR: Helps maintain a constant flow of communication needed in order for the team to achieve its goal.

EVALUATOR: Studies results and assists in making changes where needed.

Maintenance roles focus on assisting others on the team. Every individual should assume the following maintenance roles within the team.

ENCOURAGER: Works at building positive morale among team members and promotes ideas and actions of others.

FOLLOWER: Allows others to take the lead and use their abilities whenever possible.

NEGOTIATOR: Attempts to mediate conflict and is willing to compromise on issues and personal views for the benefit of the team.

PROTECTOR: Tries to shield fellow team members from outside or inside interference to achieve the team's goals.

SERVANT: Does whatever he can to meet the needs of each individual team member as the group works on its various projects.

Anti-team roles focus on self. Each team member should avoid assuming any of the following roles because they hinder team progress and success.

DOMINATOR: Tries to control conversation, ideas, and actions within the team.

BLOCKER: Delays, sidetracks, or stops progress within the team.

ATTENTION-SEEKER: Tries to get people to focus on him continually and recognize him for his accomplishments.

MEMBERS

ROLES												
PRODUCTION ROLES												
organizer												
initiator												
data collector												
facilitator												
evaluator												
MAINTENANCE ROLES												
encourager												
follower												
negotiator												
protector												
servant												
ANTI-TEAM ROLES												
dominator												
blocker												
attention-seeker												
avoider												

Figure 5. This role identification form can be used to determine the roles team members assume during team meetings. Put check marks in the columns corresponding to the roles each member (including yourself) plays most often in the group.

AVOIDER: Refuses to deal with issues, facts, and personal obligations within the team.

When forming a team, and periodically during its existence, the leader or manager should explain the foregoing team roles and encourage members to focus on production and maintenance roles. The leader should also encourage the group to watch for anti-team roles. Each team member should be committed to avoiding such roles. However, when they appear (and they will), fellow team members should quickly confront the "guilty" individual and help him return to production and maintenance roles.

"The Role Identification Form" (fig. 5) should be used periodically to have each team member evaluate how individuals relate to one another and as a team.

Chapter Summary

A team can be defined as two or more people moving along a path of interaction toward a common goal. According to this definition, it is possible to have a group working together without being a team. Every team has effective communication that centers on a well-defined common goal.

Teams are formed to allow people to accomplish more than each could working alone. A team also allows people to use their gifts, skills, and abilities more effectively. The leader should focus on developing teams of people able to compensate for one another's weaknesses.

Each team member has four key needs that must be met by fellow team members. These needs are: to use one's skills to assist the team's effort, to be accepted as part of the team, to have personal goals compatible with team goals, and to represent people and groups outside the team. These needs must be met in order for a person to feel he is making a meaningful contribution to the team.

The leader or manager must keep in mind that the team should be involved in developing and refining its goal and mission.

Participating in goal-setting gives the team a feeling of ownership which, in turn, stimulates commitment to the goal. A team will be far more effective in achieving a goal it helped develop than one imposed on it.

Team dynamics play an important part in the success or failure of a team. While involved with the group, every team member assumes one or more of the following roles: a production role, a maintenance role, or an anti-team role. Production roles focus on helping the team achieve a task or job. A maintenance role focuses on assisting others on the team. Anti-team roles focus on self and tend to reduce the productivity of others.

Personal Application

Review Ecclesiastes 4:9-13:

- Why are people more productive working in a team than by themselves?

- What should you be doing to provide more opportunity for teamwork?

Study Ephesians 4:11-12:

- What should you and other leaders in your organization be doing to better equip your people to do the work of the ministry?

- Could this be achieved more effectively through improved teamwork?

Review figure 1 and figure 2. What should you be doing to help team members major on their strengths and compensate for one another's weaknesses?

Study figure 3. Meet with your team and ask if these four key needs are being met. If not, solicit their recommendations for correcting this.

Meet with your team and ask them to evaluate their goals and determine how they could be improved.

Discuss with the team the various types of roles people assume. Have members use the form (fig. 5) to evaluate one another and determine how they will improve their working relationship.

CHAPTER 5

GOOD WORKING RELATIONSHIPS

The Bible stresses two central themes—man's relationship with God, and his relationship with his fellow man. The first four of the Ten Commandments deal with man's relationship with God, and the last six focus on his relationship with other people. From Genesis to Revelation we are constantly reminded that these relationships must be right.

It is the second of these themes, right relations with one's fellow man, that we consider now. The psalmist exclaimed, "How good and pleasant it is when brothers live together in unity!" (Ps. 133:1) Paul echoed this theme by saying, "I appeal to you, brothers, in the name of our Lord Jesus Christ, that all of you agree with one another so that there may be no divisions among you and that you may be perfectly united in mind and thought" (1 Cor. 1:10).

In light of these Scriptures, the Christian leader interested in applying biblical principles of management must work at developing and maintaining good working relationships within his group or organization.

As figure 6 illustrates, all management and leadership skills—planning, organizing, leading, staffing, and evaluating—have good working relationships as their foundation. Unfortunately, it is in

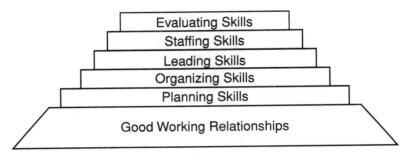

Figure 6. Good working relationships are the foundation on which all other management skills are built.

relationships that leaders are often weakest. It is important to realize that the time and effort spent planning, organizing, leading, staffing, and evaluating will be largely unproductive if the leader fails to develop and maintain good working relationships.

During a recent management seminar, one personnel director told me that approximately ninety percent of employee turnover in his company was directly associated with relationship problems.

The manager of another firm's human resources and training department agreed. "For the most part our managers are technical geniuses," she said. "Unfortunately, very few of them know how to build good working relationships in their departments." Smiling, she continued, "In fact, if things don't improve between me and my boss, I may start looking for another job."

When I first began management consulting and training, I emphasized the need for good planning, organizing, and staffing. However, over the years I have observed that the manager's number one need is to learn how to relate to his subordinates, peers, and supervisors.

Principles of Human Relationships

The leader interested in implementing a biblical model of management must apply the Bible's principles of human relationships. In the world system, self is promoted in relationships. The modern focus is on being assertive in relationships in order to get people to meet your needs. By contrast, the biblical approach is to meet the needs of others.

All relationships revolve around personal needs. Every person has needs that can be met only by forming relationships with other individuals. Even though Adam lived in a perfect geographical environment in the Garden of Eden, and though he enjoyed a perfect spiritual relationship with his Maker, God said, "It is not good for the man to be alone" (Gen. 2:18). That evaluation came as no surprise to Adam because he had needs that could only be met by forming a relationship with another person.

The leader must keep in mind that people need other people and that the function of the relationship is to insure that all needs within the relationship are met. The failure to recognize this basic principle has caused many leaders to develop serious relationship problems with others in the organization or group.

The president of a Christian organization once told me, "I would rather deal with numbers than people. When I make a mistake with numbers, all I have to do is get out my eraser, but I don't know what to do when I make a mistake with people."

Talking with some of this man's employees made it obvious that they sensed his feelings. His secretary said, "He is a very hard worker and a dedicated man—but he just doesn't seem to recognize we have needs, too."

People form relationships because they have needs that can only be met by others. For example, the president just mentioned he needed a secretary and she needed a job, so they formed a working relationship. However, in order to have a good working relationship, both the president and the secretary should have recognized their need for the other person. He needed her skills and she needed his approval.

Met needs build relationships. Meeting the needs of others is the key to developing and maintaining good working relationships. The biblical approach to leadership and management focuses on meeting the needs of people as they work at accomplishing their jobs. If the Christian leader fails to apply this principle, he or she will be plagued with relationship problems.

Unmet needs erode relationships. Just as met needs strengthen relationships, unmet needs erode them. You won't find people on their way to a divorce court because a spouse is meeting too many of their needs. It is always because too few needs are being met. The same is true in organizations. Employees get upset with supervisors because of unmet needs.

Have you ever heard an employee say, "We need a union around here because management is meeting too many of our needs"? How ridiculous! Unions are voted in because employees feel the company leadership is unwilling to meet their needs. Unmet needs always produce frustration and resentment. Met needs produce satisfaction and contentment.

Types of Relationships Found in Organizations

Human relationships within organizations, as well as in marriages and friendships, can be classified into four basic styles: *cooperation, retaliation, domination,* and *isolation.* All relationships tend to begin in a cooperation style and remain there as long as all needs are being met within the relationship. When unmet needs emerge, the relationship moves into a retaliation style. Now, one person or group is attempting to gain control over the other in order to get needs met. As soon as someone wins the struggle for control, a new relationship style develops—domination. In this style the dominator uses others to get his or her needs met. As soon as the dominated person or group realizes the situation is hopeless and their own needs will not be met, they move into an isolation style relationship. This is the last type of relationship prior to termination.

Let's examine each of these types of relationships more closely.

Conditions in a Cooperative Style Relationship

When a relationship begins, it operates in a cooperation style, marked by the following conditions:

- Mutual commitment to meet the other person's needs

- More emphasis on others than on self

- Mutual trust and respect

- Mutual use of gifts, skills, and creativity

- Joint development of solutions to problems

- Productivity in the relationship

- Continued strengthening of the relationship

Mutual commitment to meet the other person's needs. The cooperation style relationship is typified by Philippians 2:3-4: "Do nothing out of selfish ambition or vain conceit, but in humility consider others better than yourselves. Each of you should look not only to your own interests, but also to the interests of others." To avoid selfish motives and actions, we must concentrate on meeting the needs of others. (See fig. 7)

More emphasis on others than on self. The emphasis of the cooperation style is on others and their needs. This means the goal of the relationship is to serve others by meeting their needs. If each person in the relationship is applying Philippians 2:3-4, everyone's needs are being met.

Mutual trust and respect. People develop trust and respect for those who meet their needs. Therefore, people operating in a cooperation style relationship experience harmony within the group or team. People enjoy one another's company, and motives are rarely questioned.

Mutual use of gifts, skills, and creativity. The cooperation style relationship not only focuses on the work-related needs of others, but also allows others to contribute their gifts, skills, and creativity to the activities within the relationship. People never get a "left out" feeling as long as they are functioning in a cooperation relationship because they are operating at a high level of participation.

Joint development of solutions to problems. In a cooperation relationship, those involved with or affected by a problem participate in solving it. This allows the best possible solution to be implemented because people are concerned about meeting the needs of others when the problem develops.

Productivity in the relationship. The cooperation relationship is both healthy and productive. Tensions are at a minimum and energy is being used to meet needs, not quarrel over selfish interests. As a result, people experience a great deal of satisfaction by maintaining the relationship.

Personal commitment to the relationship. As people experience mutual trust and respect, use of gifts and skills, and a feeling of

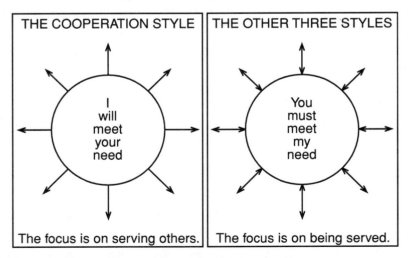

Figure 7. The cooperation style is the only one that focuses on others. The other three styles focus on self.

accomplishment, they develop strong personal commitment to the relationship. This means that the longer the relationship continues in a cooperation style, the stronger it becomes.

The cooperation relationship style emphasizes serving rather than being served. But people don't operate in a cooperation relationship at all times. Eventually a person thinks, *In this particular case, it is more important for my needs to be met than yours.* This commitment to meeting personal needs rather than the needs of others marks the beginning of the retaliation style relationship.

Conditions in a Retaliation Style Relationship

The retaliation style begins when selfishness overrides serving. From time to time all of us fall into this style of relationship by becoming more committed to getting our own needs met (or getting our own way) than meeting the needs of others.

The initial move from cooperation to retaliation frequently begins in a subtle, perhaps unnoticed, manner. However, it always comes into the open in the form of conflict. The retaliation style involves the following:

- Attempts to make others conform to what you want

- Aggressive actions toward others

- Attitudes that view the other person as an object in your way, not a person with his own needs

- Struggle for domination

- Continual conflict

- An eventual winner and loser

Attempts to make others conform to what you want. In the early stages of the retaliation style, there are subtle attempts to get the other person to give in to your wishes. However, if these covert actions are unsuccessful, stronger actions are taken.

Aggressive actions toward others. As a person becomes more self-centered, open and aggressive actions are taken in an attempt to force others to meet his needs. Leaders frequently do this by using their position to pressure people to go along with their wishes.

Attitudes that view the other person as an object in your way, not a person with his own needs. As one moves deeper into the retaliation style relationship, he becomes more and more self-centered. Eventually everyone who disagrees with him or fails to go along with his wishes is seen as a roadblock or barrier. At this point, he rapidly begins losing interest in the needs of others.

Struggle for domination. Once a person begins seeing others as barriers to getting his needs met, he attempts to dominate or control everyone else in the relationship. By this time he is truly convinced his needs, ideas, and feelings are the most important in this situation and therefore he is justified in trying to dominate others. He develops the attitude, "What is best for me is best for you."

Continual conflict. Once the struggle for domination begins, a period of conflict follows. At this phase in the retaliation style, one person is attempting to emerge as the authority figure who can control the others involved in the relationship. By controlling others, he assumes he can make sure his needs are met.

An eventual winner and loser. At some point in time, a person emerges as the dominant force in the relationship and everyone else gives in on a regular basis to his or her needs while their own needs remain unmet. At this point, the relationship takes on a new style.

It is worth repeating here that the retaliation style relationship begins out of selfish motives to get one's needs met at others' expense. The individual begins aggressive actions to force others to meet his or her needs and take retaliatory measures if they fail to comply.

Jesus condemned retaliation as follows:

The Law of Moses says, "If a man gouges out another's eye, he must pay with his own eye. If a tooth gets knocked out, knock out the tooth of the one who did it." But I say: Don't resist violence! If you are slapped on one cheek, turn the other too. If you are ordered to court, and your shirt is taken from you, give your coat too. If the military demand that you carry their gear for a mile, carry it two. Give to those who ask, and don't turn away from those who want to borrow. (Matt. 5:38-42, TLB).

Jesus seems to be saying, "Even when people take advantage of you and misuse you, don't stop serving them." Failure to apply this principle leads to self-centered, retaliation style relationship and eventually to a domination style.

Conditions in a Domination Style Relationship

In a cooperation relationship everyone voluntarily works at meeting others' needs. However, once a person wins the struggle for control and moves into a domination style, people are required to meet his needs. He rarely meets theirs.

The domination style contains the following conditions:

- "Loser" controlled by "winner"

- Loser's personality "suffocated"

- Mutual loss of respect

- Loser's creativity and skills not used

- Loser resorts to manipulation

- Loser eventually concludes situation is hopeless and stops trying to get needs met

"Loser" controlled by "winner." In a domination style relationship, the winner of the struggle for control becomes the decision-maker. Others in the relationship are required to give in to the wishes and ideas of the dominator.

Loser's personality "suffocated." As the domination style progresses, the dominator begins forcing others in the relationship to become what he wants them to be. He tries to control how others think and act and will not accept ideas contrary to his own. Eventually those being dominated are required to give up their own personalities and take on the personality the dominator wants them to have.

Mutual loss of respect. Eventually people in a domination style relationship lose respect for each other. The dominator no longer respects those he controls and no one respects him. As this occurs, concern for one another's needs also decreases.

Loser's creativity and skills not used. As the dominator loses respect for others in the relationship, he also stops caring about the skills and abilities of others and begins promoting his own skills and creativity. He makes sure the relationship focuses on what he can do and wants to do—what he is good at doing—and disregards any idea or activity that does not promote him or his skills.

Loser resorts to manipulation. Eventually those being dominated attempt to manipulate the dominator in order to get their needs met. However, manipulation never works. Instead it tends to add to the problems developing between the dominator and those being dominated. In most cases, the dominator tries to administer some type of discipline when he is manipulated in order to discourage further attempts.

Loser eventually concludes situation is hopeless and stops trying to get needs met. At this point the people being dominated feel they have been rejected and their needs will remain unmet. When this occurs, they take the first step toward a new relationship style—isolation. It is always those being dominated that initiate the move to an isolation style relationship.

Conditions in an Isolation Style Relationship

At this point the relationship is degenerating rapidly as indicated by the following conditions:

- Other person mentally blocked out

- Communication stopped

- Mutual mistrust

- Problems unsolved

- Needs unmet

- Mutual unconcern

- Productivity greatly decreased

- Relationship terminated

Other person mentally blocked out. This is the first phase of the isolation relationship. The person or people being dominated begin mentally blocking out the dominator, and thus the isolation relationship begins.

Communication stopped. Once people start mentally blocking out each other, communication breaks down. Each person involved in the relationship no longer knows what the other is thinking or feeling. Individuals become more withdrawn and isolated from one other.

Mutual mistrust. The breakdown in communication contributes to increasing mistrust within the relationship. Motives are questioned and hostility increases. At this point, everyone becomes more defensive and argumentative, with each person pointing an accusing finger at the other.

Problems unsolved. The relationship becomes consumed with problems for which there appear to be no solutions. Therefore, problems remain unsolved. No one is willing to accept responsibility for causing the problems and one individual's recommended solution is always rejected by others in the relationship.

Needs unmet. By the time a relationship reaches the isolation style, most needs go unmet. These unmet needs cause the individuals to become more and more self-centered and frustrated. As indicated earlier, unmet needs erode the relationship.

Mutual unconcern. As people become more self-centered, they develop less concern for those around them. As the relationship continues to deteriorate, each individual tends to think only of himself and his unmet needs and loses all concern for the needs of others. The individual cannot see how his own self-centeredness is hurting the others in the relationship—for he is focused only on himself. An attitude of self-pity prevails throughout the relationship.

Productivity greatly decreased. At this point the relationship is no longer productive. Needs are not being met and problems are no longer being solved. And since communication has broken down, there is not much hope that things will get better. Despair begins to set in.

Relationship terminated. In most cases the relationship is terminated at this point. Unfortunately, a relationship that started off with a mutual commitment and desire to meet the other person's needs has the potential to terminate once selfishness begins controlling the attitudes of individuals. The commitment to get one's own needs met at the expense of another is the number one destroyer of relationships. The end results can be seen by comparing the conditions in the cooperation style with those of the isolation style relationship.

Restoring Relationships to the Cooperation Style

Everyone experiences relationship problems from time to time. Therefore, it is important to know what causes such problems and how to return to a cooperative style. Many Christians have allowed themselves to be deceived into believing a godly person never has problems in relationships. Such thinking is very dangerous because it leads one to assume that if he has relationship problems, it is a sign he is not very mature spiritually.

Christians often try to suppress their problems and not bring them out into the open to be dealt with and solved. One should keep in mind that *it is the suppression of—and resulting failure to deal with—relationship problems that indicates spiritual immaturity, and not necessarily the problem itself.* The mature person faces problems when they occur and commits himself to finding a solution. On the other hand, the immature person frequently tries to ignore problems and avoids dealing with the issues involved.

Such action is not scriptural. Jesus said, "So if you are standing before the altar in the Temple, offering a sacrifice to God, and suddenly remember that a friend has something against you, leave your sacrifice there beside the altar and go and apologize and be reconciled to him, and then come and offer your sacrifice to God" (Matt. 5:23-24,TLB).

Therefore, as soon as a relationship moves out of the cooperation style, the following steps should be taken:

- Admit your current relationship style (see James 5:16).

- Admit your selfishness is sin and ask God and the others involved to forgive you (see Col. 3:13; Matt. 6:14-15).

- Make a decision to develop a cooperation style relationship (see Phil. 2:3-4).

- Begin acting out of love (see 1 Cor. 13:4-7).

- Start thanking God for those in the relationship (see 1 Thes. 5:18; James 1:2-4).

The steps listed here are seldom easy. However, God has given these principles as a means of restoring relationships to a cooperative and productive state.

Admit your current relationship style. "Admit your faults to one another" (James 5:16,TLB). This is the starting point in restoring relationships. Until a person is willing to recognize his or her contribution to the problem and admit the mistake, there is no hope of improving the relationship.

Unfortunately, it is generally easier to see the faults of others than it is to see our own. Jesus said, "Don't criticize, and then you won't be criticized. For others will treat you as you treat them. And why worry about a speck in the eye of a brother when you have a board in your own? Should you say, 'Friend, let me help you get that speck out of your eye,' when you can't even see because of the board in your own?" (Matt. 7:1-4, TLB)

In this passage Jesus makes it clear we are to focus on our own mistakes and weaknesses and not criticize others. This is the first step in returning to a cooperation style relationship.

Admit your selfishness is sin and ask God and the others involved to forgive you. In Colossians 3:13 and Matthew 6:14-15 we are told to forgive one another. This is one of the most important steps in returning to a cooperation style relationship. We must both extend forgiveness to others and ask forgiveness ourselves. Unfortunately, asking forgiveness is frequently one of the most difficult things to do, especially if we feel we are right and others are wrong.

Make a decision to develop a cooperation style relationship. In first describing the cooperation style relationship we cited Philippians 2:3-4. "Do nothing out of selfish ambition or vain conceit, but in humility consider others better than yourselves. Each of you should look not only to your own interests, but also to the interests of others." It is important to recognize it was the violation of this passage that destroyed the cooperation style. Therefore, it is the implementation of this principle that now moves the relationship back to cooperation.

Begin acting out of love (see 1 Cor. 13:4-7). These verses define love in action and focus on others rather than self. It isn't enough to tell someone you are sorry for the way you have acted. You must change your actions. This passage describes the way we should act toward others—patient and kind, never jealous or envious, never boastful or proud, never haughty or selfish or rude, for starters.

Start thanking God for those in the relationship. People are not always easy to get along with. They frequently irritate us and we would like to avoid them. One should remember that "As iron sharpens iron, so one man sharpens another" (Prov. 27:17). It is possible that our irritation points to a weakness in our own character. Scripture tells us to be thankful during trials because they help perfect us (see James 1:2-4). Therefore, it is important to thank God for people we are involved with, even when we experience relationship problems.

Rules for Right Relationships

In order to maintain a cooperation style relationship, apply the following rules:

Attack the problem, not the person. When people fail to meet our needs, we tend to attack them instead of the problem. If you attack the person instead of the problem, you will cause the relationship to move from cooperation to retaliation.

Verbalize feelings, don't act them out. State how you feel and why instead of communicating your feelings by the way you act. Acting out feelings leads to misunderstandings, resentment, and additional hurt feelings.

Forgive in place of judging. When you are wronged, forgive the person involved. Don't hold a grudge or judge the person for his actions.

Be committed to give more than you take. The key to a cooperation relationship is giving more than you take. Always focus on meeting the needs of the other person. If everyone in the relationship does this, all needs will continually be met and the relationship will remain in a cooperation style.

Jesus said, "Do not judge, and you will not be judged. Do not condemn, and you will not be condemned. Forgive, and you will be forgiven. Give, and it will be given to you" (Luke 6:37-38). If we focus on meeting the needs of others, they will in turn focus on meeting our needs.

Finally, Romans 12:9-21 provides the model for Christian conduct in personal relationships. The passage begins by stating that love should be genuine. It points out that Christians should be meeting the needs of people and even when persecuted, they should not retaliate.

Personal Application

Review the four relationship styles presented in this chapter and use them to evaluate your current relationships.

Meditate on Philippians 2:3-4 and list ways you could more effectively meet people's needs at work, home, church, and in the neighborhood.

Determine areas within your relationships where there are problems, and apply the five steps presented in this chapter for returning to a cooperation style relationship.

CHAPTER 6

PLANNING

While trying to define his job for me, the vice president of a missions organization said, "My title should be vice president in charge of fire fighting. I spend all my time running around trying to keep organizational fires from spreading." He concluded, "We don't plan it that way; it just happens."

His last statement was very true because without proper planning, things do "just happen." Unfortunately, as my friend was finding, many of these happenings tend to be undesirable and detrimental to the organization.

Lack of proper planning puts individuals and organizations on the defense instead of the offense. Like the vice-president of the mission organization, people get caught in the trap of reacting to crises rather than implementing preplanned actions. Thus they spend most of their time fighting organizational fires.

By contrast, we read in Scripture, "Any enterprise is built by wise planning, becomes strong through common sense, and profits wonderfully by keeping abreast of the facts" (Prov. 24:3-4, TLB).

A missions organization has a clearly assigned task. Jesus said, "Go into all the world and preach the Good News to all creation" (Mark

16:15). Today "all creation" consists of more than 4 billion people. And by the year 2000, there will be over 7 billion people. In order to stay even with population growth in this decade, over 62 million people must be reached with the Gospel each year. That's without any growth in the percentage rate of people calling themselves Christians.

Such a task will not be accomplished by simply fighting organizational fires. Leaders in our Christian organizations must use effective planning techniques if they are to make major contributions to world evangelization in this decade.

The Bible has a great deal to say about the planning process, and provides numerous principles concerning how planning should be done. Therefore, the Christian leader or manager should look to God's Word for guidance concerning how to plan the projects and activities needed to accomplish God's work.

Defining Planning

Planning consists of identifying the overall purpose of a project, the activities to be performed, their sequence, and the resources required to accomplish them. If any of these four elements is missing, plans will have less chance for success.

The Starting Point: God Has a Plan for You

The Christian leader's planning process is unique in that it starts with the realization that God has a plan and purpose for the Christian organization and its people. "'For I know the plans I have for you,' declares the Lord, 'plans to prosper you and not to harm you, plans to give you hope and a future'" (Jer. 29:11). God also says, "I will instruct you and teach you in the way you should go; I will counsel you and watch over you" (Ps. 32:8). To Jeremiah God said, "Before I formed you in the womb I knew you, before you were born I set you apart; I appointed you as a prophet to the nations" (Jer. 1:5).

In these passages and many others, God makes it clear He has a plan for people. Therefore, the first step in the planning process is to recognize that fact and seek God's guidance.

However, because God does have plans for organizations and individuals, some people use this as a cop-out for not planning. The chairman of one church board told me he thought it was a sin to plan. "Why plan?" he asked, "I know God is in control, so I'm just trusting Him."

My question is, "For what?"

On the other hand, some Christian leaders feel they must do it all. They not only plan every detail, but also think they must produce the results. There is no place for this type of thinking in a Christian organization. Paul makes this point clear by saying, "I planted the seed, Apollos watered it, but God made it grow" (1 Cor. 3:6).

The Christian leader must realize his job is to determine the actions God wants him to take and then trust God for the results. As the Bible says again, "Many are the plans in a man's heart, but it is the Lord's purpose that prevails" (Prov. 19:21).

God Is the Source of Power to Achieve Plans

Once the Christian leader recognizes that God has a plan, the next step is to realize God is the source of power to accomplish the plan. This principle is reflected in Hebrews 11:32-34. "I do not have time to tell about Gideon, Barak, Samson, Jephthah, David, Samuel and the prophets, who through faith conquered kingdoms, administered justice, and gained what was promised; who shut the mouths of lions, quenched the fury of the flames, and escaped the edge of the sword; whose weakness was turned to strength; and who became powerful in battle and routed foreign armies."

Undoubtedly many hours of planning went into the aforementioned achievements. However, this passage makes it clear the plans were based on faith in God to produce the results. For truly, "In his heart a man plans his course, but the Lord determines his steps" (Prov. 16:9). Therefore, the Christian leader must first recognize God has a plan and prayerfully seek it. Once the plans are formalized and executed, he must trust God for the results.

Planning Begins by Identifying the Purpose

Earlier, planning was defined as the process of identifying the overall purpose of the project, the activities to be performed, their sequence, and the resources required. The first part of the definition deals with identifying the purpose, and this is where all planning should begin.

Purpose deals with the question why in such matters as:

Why is this important?

Why should I get involved?

Why do we need these things done?

Why should this be top priority?

Defining the purpose motivates people to unite behind a cause. Jesus always recruited people to a cause or purpose—not a job or plan. He assigned jobs only after people joined the cause. For example, Jesus began His ministry by saying to potential disciples, "Come, follow Me . . . and I will make you fishers of men" (Matt. 4:19).

Jesus clearly stated the purpose to those following Him. He ended His ministry by sharing some of the details of how His purpose was to be achieved. "Therefore go and make disciples of all nations" (Matt. 28:19).

Nehemiah told his coworkers the purpose for rebuilding the wall around the city of Jerusalem. "You see the trouble we are in: Jerusalem lies in ruins, and its gates have been burned with fire. Come, let us rebuild the wall of Jerusalem, and we will no longer be in disgrace" (Neh. 2:17).

God explained the purpose when he asked Noah to build an ark for his family and the animals (see Gen. 6:9-22). In other words, he answered Noah's questions concerning why. This principle is seen throughout the Bible. Yet it is frequently overlooked as important to the planning process.

Planning is hard work, so it can be very discouraging. This is why it is important to begin the planning process by identifying the overall purpose of the function or project being planned. A strong sense of purpose helps develop the conviction and commitment needed for the work of planning. If the purpose is not understood, planning may be considered "just more busywork" by those involved.

A member of a church board once told me annual planning meetings in his church were a waste of time. "I don't know why we have these meetings," he said. "All we do is decide to keep doing what we've been doing. The trouble is, no one knows why we started all these programs to begin with." Unfortunately, all too many planning sessions serve little purpose. Unless the purpose of the function is clearly understood, an activity can become a traditional ritual performed unconsciously.

Therefore, every planning session should begin by answering the question, "Why are we doing this?" The answer to that question represents the purpose. And if the purpose is meeting a real need, people will see the value of getting involved in the planning.

Develop a Vision of the Completed Plan

The vision—a mental picture of the completed plan—stimulates action, innovation, and creativity. Like the purpose or cause, a vision motivates people to make a strong commitment to the project. It also helps develop group unity and personal conviction and justifies the expenditure of resources in achieving the goal.

Before his battle with Goliath, David visualized the end result. "You come to me with a sword and a spear, but I come to you in the name of the Lord of the armies of heaven and of Israel—the very God Whom you have defied. Today the Lord will conquer you and I will kill you and cut off your head; and then I will give the dead bodies of *your* men to the birds and wild animals; and the whole world will know that there is a God in Israel!" (1 Sam. 17:45-46,TLB)

Visualizing the end result before going into battle helped David both to plan his attack on Goliath and to determine the steps needed for accomplishing his plan.

David also indicated he knew the purpose of the battle with Goliath: "And Israel will learn that the Lord does not depend on weapons to fulfill His plans" (v. 47, TLB). Understanding the purpose of the battle motivated David to action. Visualizing the end result helped him form his battle plan. And even though David was the one carrying out the steps of the plan, it is clear he was trusting God for the results.

Develop Measurable Objectives

The next step in the planning process involves setting *measurable* objectives. A measurable objective tells exactly *what* will be accomplished, *how much* is to be accomplished, and *when* it will be completed. It is important to keep in mind that an objective must be measurable to be manageable.

Before the rebuilding of the wall of Jerusalem, King Artaxerxes asked Nehemiah two important questions that required the formation of a measurable objective. "What is it you want?" (Neh. 2:4) "How long will your journey take?" (v. 6) These questions helped clarify the objective in terms of what, how much, and when. In other words, the objective became measurable.

Without measurable objectives, an organization has no way to evaluate performance. For example, suppose your church developed the following objectives: "We will raise more money for missions." This is a poorly stated objective because performance cannot be effectively evaluated. The objective states what is to occur (raise more money for missions), but it does not tell how much more will be raised or when it will be achieved.

To make the objective measurable, restate it as follows: "This year (when) we will raise 20 percent (how much) more money for missions (what) than we did last year." Now the organization can effectively evaluate the progress being made toward achieving its missions budget goal because it knows how much increase is expected within a given period of time.

This approach to setting objectives helps leaders and managers be more specific in planning. It removes planning from the realm of vague ideas and helps people state specifically what is to occur within a predetermined time frame.

The Value of Measurable Objectives

Measurable objectives give meaning to faith. Without measurable objectives, people tend to talk and plan in generalities. They profess to be "trusting God to lead," but do not know where they are headed and are unable to determine when they have arrived. On the other hand, measurable objectives focus on exactly what one believes God will do, how much a person is trusting God for, and when it will occur. Measurable objectives bring faith into focus, giving it meaning and an identity.

Measurable objectives help people know what to pray for. During a management seminar, Canadian businessman Will Shavers told how measurable objectives helped his prayer time become more meaningful. "Before I started setting measurable objectives, I prayed, 'God bless my business.' But now that I have these objectives, I know exactly what and how much to ask of God and when to expect results."

It is difficult to know when God has answered the prayer, "Bless my business." However, when we take the time to set measurable objectives, our prayers begin focusing on what we want God to do, how much we want accomplished, and when we expect it to be done.

Developing Good Objectives

A good objective is always accomplishable. Every objective should be accomplishable. If people realize it is impossible to reach the goal in the time allotted, they become frustrated and tend to lose their interest in, and commitment to, the project. Therefore, when developing measurable objectives, always make sure they are within the realm of possibility.

A good objective is always realistic. Sometimes even when it is possible to accomplish a stated objective, it may not be realistic to do so. For example, an organization might develop an objective that could be accomplished by expanding its facilities. But if facility expansion is not a realistic option due to excessive interest rates on loans needed for the expansion project, then the objective is not a good one. Therefore, it is important to make sure objectives are realistic as well as accomplishable.

A good objective is always compatible with other organizational goals. Each objective within an organization should contribute to the overall purpose or cause. For example, if one department's objectives do not contribute to the organization's objectives, they are not compatible; they are in conflict because they do not contribute to a common purpose.

A good objective is always motivational. Good objectives stimulate interest and commitment. Good objectives provide the spark that ignites people to action. It the objectives are not motivational, the plans will have little chance to succeed—for people are reluctant to commit themselves to something that they don't really want to be involved in. Therefore, developing objectives that are motivational is one of the more important tasks of successful planning.

Identify the Activities Needed to Accomplish the Objective.

As indicated earlier in the chapter, the purpose answers questions concerning *why* the plan is important and needed. Objectives explain specifically *what* is to be achieved and *when*. And the activities focus on *how* the plan is to be accomplished.

Participation is the key to developing good activities. People responsible for carrying out an activity should participate in its development because they usually are more knowledgeable about how it should be performed. Therefore, during this phase of the planning process, the leader should make sure everyone in his or her group is involved in developing the activities required to achieve the department's or team's objectives.

Participation gives people "ownership" of the plans. People who are required to carry out activities without participation in the development generally lack motivation and commitment to make the plans succeed. On the other hand, people involved in developing an activity tend to take more pride in their work.

I was made aware of the importance of ownership when we moved to Colorado Springs. A real estate salesman took my wife and me on a tour of the city to look at houses. One afternoon we drove through a well-kept neighborhood. The homes had beautifully landscaped yards with a profusion of trees and shrubs, and each house appeared to have a new coat of paint.

However, as we drove along we came to a place in poor repair. Even though the house appeared to have been built at the same time as the others, the grass had dried up, limbs broken from trees were lying in the yard, the screen door was hanging lopsided on its hinges, and the paint was peeling off the house.

As I studied the run-down condition of the property, the real estate salesman said, "You can buy that house for about $5,000 under market value."

I frowned and asked, "Why would anyone let a nice house deteriorate like that?"

"Oh, it's simple," the realtor replied. The people living there are renters. The owners moved to California four years ago."

As we drove on, I was reminded that people have less commitment to things they don't own. Then it occurred to me, the same is true in organizations. If people don't feel ownership of the plans and activities of the organization, they frequently react like the renters of a house—they tend to lack pride, motivation, and commitment.

People develop a feeling of ownership in the planning process only when they participate in developing the purpose, objectives, and activities. When they are involved, people will work hard to succeed because the plans belong to them.

Innovation and creativity should be encouraged when developing the activities. This is an excellent time in the planning process to encourage innovation and creativity. The leader or manager should ask those under his supervision to develop the best possible activities for achieving the objective in the most productive and effective way possible.

Innovation and creativity keep people and their plans from becoming stagnant. Therefore, when developing activities, people should be encouraged to improve on traditional methods and processes. They should be asked to look for new and improved ways of performing even routine tasks and activities.

Jim Penrose, the owner of a small business, decided to involve all his employees in planning the activities needed to achieve the company's objectives. He describes what happened when he encouraged his employees to be innovative. "At first it was scary. I felt I was losing control because people started coming up with new ideas and different ways of getting things done. However, I soon realized my people frequently knew more about how things should be done than I did. Though I was reluctant at first to let them determine how we would do some of the jobs, once I saw the results, I was sold on the idea!"

Some of his employees later told me they had considered looking for new jobs before Jim started encouraging them to get involved in helping with the planning. One of the employees said with a smile, "Mr. Penrose couldn't run me off with a club now."

During World War II, Soichiro Honda's business in Japan was completely destroyed by American bombers. Following the war he started over, manufacturing motorcycles and then automobiles. The Honda company grew to become one of the largest automobile manufacturing firms in Japan, with approximately 50,000 employees.

When asked how he developed such a successful company, Soichiro Honda said, "The thinking for the corporation is done by everyone—including assembly line workers." Honda turned the innovative ideas of all his employees into successful plans and productive results.

Place Activities in Proper Sequence

Once the activities have been identified, the next step is to place them in proper sequence, making sure each activity is performed at the proper time. The right activity performed at the wrong time can be just as devastating as conducting the wrong activity altogether.

Identifying the activities describes how the plan will be carried out. Placing the activity in proper sequence tells where it fits in a series of events.

Determine the Resources Needed to Achieve the Plan

The planning process is not complete until the resources needed to achieve the plan have been determined. Jesus pointed out the importance of determining the resources needed and available when planning a project or activity. He asked two important questions that required thorough resource planning to answer. "Suppose one of you wants to build a tower. Will he not first sit down and estimate the cost to see if he has enough money to complete it?" (Luke 14:28) "Or suppose a king is about to go to war against another king. Will he not first sit down and consider whether he is able with 10,000 men to oppose the one coming against him with 20,000?" (v. 31)

It is important to keep in mind that resource planning is a very major and important part of the overall planning process. It is also important to note that, in the planning process, identifying the resources needed follows placing activities in their proper sequence. The sequence of activities will have an effect on the type of resources required and when they will be needed.

There are six key factors to be considered when allocating resources for a plan:

- People

- Space

- Equipment

- Supplies

- Time

- Money

Are you viewing people as your most valuable and important resource in achieving the plan? As pointed out in Chapter 2, people are an organization's most valuable resource. Therefore, they should be considered first when identifying resources needed to achieve a plan. When determining the people needed, the following questions should be answered:

What type of skills, gifts, and abilities are needed to pursue each of the activities?

Do we currently have people with these skills in the organization?

Do we have people interested in developing the skills needed?

If we need to go outside the organization to find the skills, how will we proceed?

What type of facility and how much space will be needed to pursue the activities? Facilities and space play an important role in the accomplishment of plans. Scheduling of facility and space use are the most frequently overlooked aspects of resource planning. Unfortunately, it is also one of the most important parts of the planning process. All activities require space and facilities. If such space is not made available, the best of planned activities may fail.

What type of equipment is needed, and is it available? Like facility and space use, equipment also plays an important role in achieving the plan. Frequently, each activity requires different equipment. Therefore, it is important to place the activity in its proper time sequence in order to know when and for how long to schedule the needed equipment.

What type of supplies will be needed and how much? Most production managers are aware of the importance of supplies in achieving any plan. Acquiring and distributing supplies frequently consumes a considerable amount of time. Therefore, adequate attention should be given to making sure the type and quantity of supplies are available as needed. On large projects this is a full-time job.

How much time will be required to prepare for and execute each activity? The time it takes to prepare for and execute each activity will determine how long it takes to accomplish each overall plan. The amount of people, space, equipment, and supplies available will greatly influence the amount of time required for each activity.

How much money will be needed to accomplish each activity in sequence? The amount of money needed is determined by the quantity and type of resources used. At the same time, the amount of money available will determine what can be purchased.

Satan always tries to convince the Christian leader or manager there are not enough resources to accomplish the job. People involved in resource planning should keep in mind that if the plans are in accordance with God's will for the individual and/or organization, He will provide the resources to accomplish the activities.

Summary of the Planning Process

As we have seen, there are six stages in the planning process as outlined below:

Prerequisites: Before starting the planning process, prerequisites should be met:

a. Recognize God has a plan for you and your organization.

b. Recognize God is the source of power to achieve the plan.

Stage One: Identify the purpose of the project or activity.

a. The purpose tells why the plan is important.

b. The purpose develops conviction and commitment to the plan.

Stage Two: Visualize the plan completed.

a. Visualizing the plan completed builds confidence and faith in the project and purpose.

b. It also speeds up the planning process.

Stage Three: Develop measurable objectives.

a. Objectives tell what will be accomplished.

b. Objectives tell how much will be achieved and when.

Stage Four: Identify the activities needed to accomplish the objectives.

a. Activities explain how the objectives will be achieved.

b. This phase of the planning process should focus on participation, innovation, and creativity.

Stage Five: Place the activities in proper sequence. This stage explains where each activity fits in the overall plan.

Stage Six: Determine the resources needed to achieve the plan.

When considering resources needed, one must look at people, space, equipment, supplies, time, and money.

The amount of resources needed will depend on the activities to be performed and their sequence.

The Storyboard: An Excellent Planning Tool

The storyboard (see fig. 8) is an excellent planning tool because it helps visualize the parts of the plan as they are being formulated. It was first used in the movie industry to help lay out the sequence of scenes for a film. The storyboard is now used by hotel and restaurant chains, various corporations, educational institutions, and international Christian organizations.

The storyboard serves the planning process in the following ways:

• It aids the brainstorming process.

• It helps keep attention on the topic under discussion.

• It helps organize functions and activities in proper sequence.

• It stimulates innovation and creativity.

Pat Yanney, one the office managers for The Navigators, recently told me, "Using storyboards has greatly increased our productivity during planning sessions." He went on to explain, "We are now getting more creative ideas out of our staff, better organized plans in much more detail, and our people are more excited about the hard work that goes into the planning process."

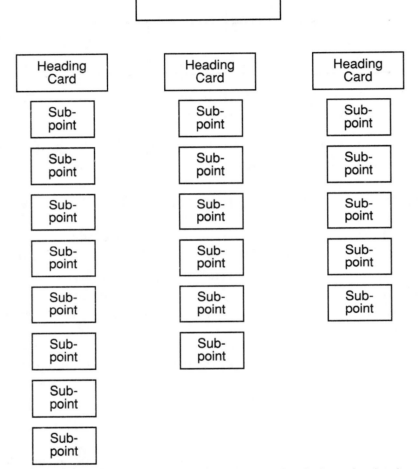

Figure 8. The storyboard resembles a bulletin board in design. Cards are pinned on the board showing the topic being discussed or planned. Heading cards show the major parts under discussion and sub-point cards show the various sctivities under each function.

Planning is basically the process of generating and organizing ideas. The storyboard stimulates the generation of ideas and allows them to be visualized and arranged in any sequence desired. It helps people focus on the topic being planned. It also provides a visual image of the plan as its various components are developed and placed in proper sequence. In other words, it tells the story of the plan.

How to Use the Storyboard in the Planning Process

As indicated in figure 8, the storyboard resembles a bulletin board. It can be constructed out of cork or any material that allows pins to be stuck in it easily. The storyboard can be any size, the larger the better. Many organizations cover an entire wall with cork or fabra-cork, a cork material used in construction of storyboards.

The use of cards. Three basic card sizes are needed when using a storyboard. The largest card (an 8 1/2-by-11-inch sheet of typing paper) is used for the topic card. The next largest card (approximately 5-by-7 inches) is used for the major heading being discussed or planned. The smallest card (3-by-5 inches) is used to record subpoint activities for each of the headings (see fig. 8).

The brainstorming process. Brainstorming is used to generate ideas for the storyboard. The purpose of brainstorming is to generate as many ideas relating to a given subject as possible. During the brain-storming session, the ideas are written on the appropriate card (topic, heading, or subpoint) and placed on the storyboard as shown in figure 8. All ideas are recorded without discussion of their value.

Evaluating the ideas. Once the brainstorming session is over, each idea on the storyboard is evaluated in terms of validity, order of sequence, and location in the plan. Those ideas determined invalid are removed from the storyboard. The location of others may need to be changed, depending on where they fit in the overall plan.

A few months ago, I used the storyboard in a consulting session with the administrative staff of a West Coast restaurant chain. The president remarked, "I am amazed at the amount of work we are accomplishing with this process. I didn't realize our people had so many good ideas."

After learning to use the storyboard as a planning tool the owner of a Colorado-based construction company said, "Using a storyboard allows us to visualize a whole project being planned from start to finish. The movable cards make organizing the plan easier and allows for schedule changes without having to rework the whole plan." The leader interested in more effective and productive planning in less time should consider using the storyboard. It is an extremely effective tool for involving people in the planning process.

Chapter Summary

Planning consists of identifying the overall purpose of a project, the activities to be performed, their sequence, and the resources required to accomplish them. For the Christian leader, planning begins by recognizing that God has a plan for the individual and will provide the power to achieve it.

Planning is hard work and can be very frustrating. It is a mental process in which people identify objectives, develop activities to achieve the objectives, determine the order in which activities will occur, and then decide what resources will be needed. Planning always deals with the future, which at times can be totally unpredictable.

Those individuals being affected by the plan should be asked for their input in the plan's development. The storyboard is an excellent tool for getting people involved in the planning process. It stimulates innovation, participation, and increased effectiveness as plans are being developed.

Personal Application

On your next planning project try following the six-stage planning process.

Experiment with the storyboard as a planning tool.

CHAPTER 7

DECISION-MAKING AND PROBLEM-SOLVING

Planning and decision-making go hand in hand. The planning process involves the most important and far-reaching decisions a leader of manager can make. In fact, the entire planning process consists of a series of interrelated decisions. The quality of any plans depends on how good the decisions are that make up the plans.

All people in leadership positions have one thing in common—they are continually required to make decisions affecting others as well as themselves. Business corporations spend hundreds of millions of dollars gathering and analyzing data in an attempt to make the best possible decisions. However, Ford Motor Company's Edsel was a classic example of how even large corporations sometimes make the wrong choice.

The big question, then, is "How does one go about making the right decisions?" The Bible gives the answer. "Where is the man who fears the Lord? God will teach him how to choose the best" (Ps. 25:12, TLB). God wants to teach His people how to make the right decisions at the right time.

Knowing God's Will—The Foundation for Decision-Making

The Christian leader's decision-making process is unique in that it is based on the realization that God does have a specific plan for him or her and that plan can be known. Therefore, in order to make right decisions, the Christian manager or leader must understand how to know God's will.

Many Christian leaders and businesspeople are frustrated and confused concerning God's will for them and their organizations or businesses. On numerous occasions I have been told, "I would gladly do God's will if I could just figure it out."

One frustrated Christian businessman recently told me, "I feel God is playing a game of hide-and-seek with me. I want to do His will, but He won't tell me what it is." He shook his head and went on, "How can I do what God wants if He doesn't let me know?"

The Process of Knowing God's Will

God does not play "hide-and-seek" with us concerning His will. The Bible gives us a simple process for knowing God's will. But often we don't know God's will because we don't spend enough time studying God's Word.

The problem is that most of us aren't listening to God and therefore don't understand what He says. Many people seem to think that God communicates His will through supernatural or unnatural means, such as a voice from heaven, a special vision, or an event like the parting of the Red Sea. Even though God has occasionally used special or spectacular means to communicate His will, that is not His standard practice. Jesus made that point clear when talking to the scribes and Pharisees who were seeking a special sign (see Matt. 12:38-39).

Elijah also learned that God doesn't need supernatural means to communicate His will. In 1 Kings 19:11-12 we read, "Then a great and powerful wind tore the mountains apart and shattered the rocks before the Lord, but the Lord was not in the wind. After the wind there was an earthquake, but the Lord was not in the earthquake. After the earthquake came a fire, but the Lord was not in the fire. And after the fire came a gentle whisper." Elijah learned that God speaks through a "gentle whisper," not necessarily through spectacular events.

In order to know God's will, you must first be committed to doing it. I have never met a non-Christian who knew exactly what decisions God wanted him to make. God doesn't waste His time communicating His will to people not interested in doing it. This is clearly seen in Romans 12:1-2: "Therefore, I urge you, brothers, in view of God's mercy to offer your bodies as living sacrifices, holy and pleasing to God . . . Do not conform any longer to the pattern of this world, but be transformed by the renewing of your mind. Then you will be able to test and approve what God's will is—His good, pleasing and perfect will."

In this passage Paul points out that we find God's will only after we have committed ourselves to God. He also explains that God's will for us is good and pleasing and, in fact, perfect. Paul was able to make the right decisions and accomplish great things because he met the prerequisite for knowing the "good, pleasing, and perfect" will of God—he was totally committed to doing it.

Recognize God has a specific plan for you and your organization or business. This is the second step in the process of knowing God's will. Throughout the Bible God makes it clear He has a specific plan for His people. "'For I know the plans I have for you', declares the Lord, 'plans to prosper you and not to harm you, plans to give you hope and a future'" (Jer. 29:11). "I will instruct you and teach you in the way you should go; I will counsel you and watch over you" (Ps. 32:8). If we have committed ourselves to God, He will communicate His will to us. The big question is, "*How* does He tell us what He wants done?"

God communicates His will by giving us a desire to do what He wants done. "For it is God who works in you to will and to act according to His good purpose" (Phil. 2:13). God promises to put His will in us and then gives us the power or resources to achieve it.

When I first ran across this verse I asked myself, *How does God put His will in me?* I began to realize, if I have the will to do something, it is in the form of a desire. Realizing this reminded me of God's promise: "Delight yourself in the Lord and He will give you the desires of your heart" (Ps. 37:4).

This verse tells us that if we are committed to God and His will, He will give us the desires of our heart. This promise parallels the one in Philippians 2:13. Therefore, if I am really committed to doing God's will, I should begin examining the desires of my heart.

If the desire is God's will, we will have peace about doing it and the power to achieve it. Many people say, "Oh, you can't trust your desires to be from God. Satan tempts us with evil desires, so you can't know if they come from God or the Devil." Scripture doesn't say, "God will give you every desire of your heart." Instead, the promise is conditional. If we meet the prerequisite of being totally committed to God and His will for us, then God will give us the desires of our heart because, according to Philippians 2:13, He put them there.

Notice too that if the desire is from God, He will make sure it is fulfilled. In other words, He will not only give you the desire, He will provide the power and resources to make sure the desire is met. This is one way to determine if the desire is from God. If we have the desire, but never acquire the resources or means to meet the desire, we can conclude the desire was not from God.

However, it is possible to have both the desire and resources to meet it and still not be in God's will. That is where Isaiah 26:3 comes in. "You will keep in perfect peace him whose mind is steadfast, because he trusts in You." God promises us peace as long as we are operating in His will. Therefore, if we have a desire and the resources to accomplish it but do not have peace about the decision, we can conclude we should not pursue it. Any desire that is God's will is accompanied by the resources to achieve it and the peace to pursue it.

Checklist for Knowing God's Will

There are four key questions to ask in order to determine God's will in a decision-making situation.

- Am I committed to doing God's will in this situation? (Rom. 12:1-2)

- Are the desires of my heart to pursue this particular course? (Ps. 37:4)

- Does God provide the power and resources to accomplish the desire? (Phil. 2:13)

- Does God give me peace to continue working on the project and to make the necessary decisions to achieve it? (Isa. 26:3)

The Bible's Five-Step Decision-Making Process

Step One: Correctly diagnose the issue or problem. If the issue or problem is not correctly diagnosed, the decision will be wrong because it was made on false assumptions. This principle is illustrated in the account of Moses sending out the twelve spies.

God had already made it clear that He was giving the land of Canaan to the people of Israel (see Num. 13:1-2). The purpose of the spies' trip was to ascertain the type of people, cities, land, and produce that were in their new homeland (vv. 17-20).

However, the majority of the spies incorrectly diagnosed the issue. They spied out the land to evaluate their ability to conquer its inhabitants. But that was not the issue. God had already said He was giving the land to the people of Israel. As a result of the spies' misinterpretation, they decided they were unable to take the land because of the size and power of the people living within the walled cities. By incorrectly diagnosing the issue or problem, the majority of the spies made the wrong decision.

Recently while I was discussing this aspect of the decision-making process at a management seminar, a businessman disgustedly commented, "I am currently recovering from that very mistake. I failed to clarify a problem with my architect. As a result we made several wrong decisions on a shopping center we were developing." He went on to say, "And each wrong decision cost us several thousand dollars."

Both the people of Israel and the businessman at the seminar learned that if a person fails to diagnose the issues correctly, the decisions will be wrong and costly.

Step Two: Gather and analyze the facts. "Any enterprise is built by wise planning, becomes strong through common sense, and profits wonderfully by keeping abreast of the facts" (Prov. 24: 3-4, TLB). As this Scripture suggests, gathering and analyzing facts plays an important part in the decision-making process. Proverbs 18:13 says it even stronger: "What a shame—yes, how stupid!—to decide before knowing the facts!" (TLB)

When gathering and analyzing facts, the following questions should be answered:

- *What does the Bible say on the matter?* There is great value and reward in knowing and applying God's Word. "Do not let this Book of the Law depart from your mouth; meditate on it day and night, so that you may be careful to do everything written in it. Then you will be prosperous and successful" (Josh. 1:8).

- *What does God tell me when I pray?* "Call to Me and I will answer you and tell you great and unsearchable things you do not know" (Jer. 33:3).

- *Am I committed to doing the will of God in this situation?* Earlier in the chapter we saw that we are to be committed to doing God's will in order to know His will (see Rom. 12:1-2).

- *What are my interests and desires in this situation?* "Delight yourself in the Lord and He will give you the desires of your heart" (Ps. 37:4).

- *What counsel do I get from people in this situation?* "For lack of guidance a nation falls, but many advisers make victory sure" (Prov. 11:14).

- *What do conditions and circumstances indicate in this situation?* As we read once before, "Any enterprise is built by wise planning, becomes strong through common sense, and profits wonderfully by keeping abreast of the facts" (Prov. 24:3-4,TLB).

Before developing possible alternatives, the Christian leader, manager, or business person should answer these six key questions. These questions help gather facts and information needed to make the right decision.

Step Three: Develop alternatives. After the facts have been gathered and analyzed, the next step is the development of alternatives. Important decisions should never be made until several alternatives have been developed. Without alternatives to consider, the manager or leader chooses the first possible solution. And the first choice may not be the best.

Developing alternatives forces the leader to evaluate all of the data and facts and take time to think through the various options. It also helps him avoid the temptation to solve problems quickly. For many managers this is one of their greatest weaknesses in decision-making.

"It is not good to have zeal without knowledge, nor to be hasty and miss the way" (Prov. 19:2). This verse certainly applies to the decision-making process. The person who hurriedly chooses the first option that appears frequently misses his way. The more alternatives the leader develops, the greater his likelihood of making the right decision.

Step Four: Evaluate alternatives pro and con. Once the alternatives have been developed, each should be evaluated in terms of its strengths and weaknesses, or pros and cons. This step becomes a self-eliminating process for some of the alternatives.

Luke 14:31-32 provides a classic biblical example of this principle as taught by Jesus. "What king would ever dream of going to war without first sitting down with his counselors and discussing whether his army of 10,000 is strong enough to defeat the 20,000 men who are marching against him? If the decision is negative, then while the enemy troops are still far away, he will send a truce team to discuss terms of peace" (TLB).

This passage points out the importance of evaluating the options in terms of their positive and negative impact. A negative evaluation means a no decision. On the other hand, a positive evaluation means a possible decision.

Step Five: Select from among the positive alternatives. This may seem like a logical next step. However, it is frequently the most difficult. Many leaders and managers admit they procrastinate when it comes to decision-making because they are not sure if they are really making the best choice. One Christian executive told me, "When it comes time to make the decision, I am usually tempted to decide not to decide."

When making the selection from among alternatives, the Christian leader should keep in mind God's promise: "I will instruct you and teach you in the way you should go; I will counsel you and watch over you" (Ps. 32:8). He should also consider Isaiah 26:3: "You will keep in perfect peace him whose mind is steadfast, because he trusts in You."

Understanding the Climate within Which Decisions Are Made

A certain climate always surrounds the decision-making process. Every manager should be aware of the elements of this climate and understand their impact on the decision-making process. The elements of the decision-making climate are:

- The need for action

- Degenerating conditions as action is delayed

- Insufficient data

- The element of risk

- The consequences of failure

- The rewards of success

- The existence of more than one workable solution

The need for action. Decisions result from a need for action. As the leader or manager goes through the decision-making process, he should ask himself, *Is there a need for action?* If the answer is yes, then there is a need for a decision. On the other hand, if the answer is no, a decision might be premature.

Conditions degenerate as needed action is delayed. If no decision is made when action is needed, conditions degenerate. As conditions degenerate, the leader is put under pressure to make a decision. As pressure increases, the possibility of making the right decision decreases. Therefore, in order to make good decisions and keep conditions from degenerating, the decision should be made as close as possible to the time action is needed.

Insufficient data. In every decision-making situation, it is true that additional data, facts, and information could have been gathered and used. One never has the luxury of having all the facts when making decisions. As a result, many leaders and managers are reluctant to make decisions because they feel they have insufficient data, regardless of how much information is available.

Therefore, researching information must be kept in balance in the decision-making process. The "insufficient data trap" can lead to procrastination, which in turn causes degenerating conditions and potentially poor decisions.

The element of risk. The leader has no way of knowing the actual results of his decision. That means each decision contains an element of risk. Some leaders are reluctant to take risks, and as a result, have problems making decisions. The good decision-maker learns to calculate risks and make them work for him in the decision-making process.

When evaluating alternatives, the leader should consider the risks involved in each potential decision. However, he should not try to eliminate all risk. The best decision is not necessarily the alternative with the least risk. As a general rule, risks decrease as facts and information increases.

The consequences of failure. The greater the consequences of failure, the stronger the feeling of risk. No one likes to fail. The fear of failure greatly inhibits the decision-making process. Therefore, the leader cannot allow himself to dwell on the consequences of failure when faced with the need to make a decision. He must accept the fact that failure is always a possibility, but he must not consider it a probability when making decisions.

The rewards of success. Every leader, manager, and business person knows his success depends on his ability to make good decisions. Just as there can be severe consequences for making the wrong decision, there can be great rewards for the right one. Success is never automatic. It is always the result of making the right decision at the right time. Therefore, in every decision-making situation, the possibility of success becomes the motivating drive behind the decision made.

The existence of more than one workable solution. In most cases, more than one alternative will work. Many leaders struggle with decision-making because they feel they must find the one right decision. In reality, a poor decision properly implemented frequently works better than a good decision poorly implemented. Therefore, the leader must give as much emphasis to implementation as he does to the selection of alternatives.

Important Distinctions

Decision-making can be defined as choosing between alternatives, whereas problem-solving is the process of formulating and implementing a plan of action to eliminate a difficulty. The problem-solving process always involves making decisions. However, simply making a decision does not necessarily solve the problem.

Equating problem-solving with decision-making is a common false assumption. I have frequently heard managers say after making a decision, "Well, that solves the problem."

My response is, "You may have made a decision, but you haven't necessarily solved the problem." Decision-making is a mental process; problem-solving involves implementing and carrying out decisions in such a manner that the difficulty is eliminated.

It is also important to understand the difference between problems and conditions. A problem can be solved over a fairly short period of time. On the other hand, a condition is a currently uncontrollable circumstance superimposed on the situation from the outside. Generally, a considerable length of time is required to change conditions noticeably.

Assuming that conditions are problems creates frustrations, confusion, and low morale. Recently, in consulting with a federal agency, I was told Congress had imposed a hiring freeze on the organization. In addition, the agency was being required to double its productivity even though it could not add personnel.

The agency's project manager commented, "Our problem is we don't have enough people to handle the increased workload."

"That is not the problem—it's a condition," I explained.

He gave me a puzzled look, and I went on to explain that since Congress had imposed this situation on the agency and the matter was beyond their control, this was a condition he and his people had to live with for the time being. I also explained that the condition had created several problems that could be solved. However, it was a waste of time to keep fighting the condition because that would not change until Congress lifted the hiring freeze.

If a person mistakes a condition for a problem, he finds himself working on an uncontrollable situation. As a result, he becomes frustrated, confused, and discouraged because he fails to get results from the time and energy expended. Instead of banging one's head against an uncontrollable condition, the leader should identify the problems created by the condition and work at solving them. As stated earlier, problems can usually be solved rather quickly, but conditions are superimposed, are outside the manager's control, and generally change slowly.

The Problem-Solving Process

Problem-solving and decision-making go hand in hand. Problem-solving requires a method of eliminating a difficulty. The following problem-solving process has been used successfully by leaders and businesspeople in a wide variety of organizations and situations:

- First, determine if the situation is a problem or condition

- Clearly state the problem

- Determine what will be gained or lost in solving the problem

- Identify alternative methods and solutions

- State the cost of each alternative

- Choose between alternatives

- Delegate action steps and begin implementation

- Evaluate progress

First, determine if the situation is a problem or condition. If it is a condition, then identify the problems created by the condition and proceed with the problem-solving process. Don't try to change the condition immediately.

Clearly state the problem. Many problems are never solved because they have not been properly defined. The person who can correctly identify the problem is well on the road to solving it. False assumptions produce wrong conclusions. And wrong conclusions usually generate bigger problems. Therefore, the leader should get as much input as possible to make sure the problem is correctly identified. This is especially important if the leader becomes emotionally involved in the problem. Emotions tend to distort reality. Therefore, the more emotionally involved the leader becomes, the greater the need for outside assistance and input in determining the real problem.

Determine what will be gained or lost in solving the problem. This is an important step in the problem-solving process. For example, will solving the problem produce a better working environment, more productivity, better employee morale? Or is it possible that solving this problem will create a bigger one?

Identify alternative methods and solutions. Just as there is usually more than one workable decision, there is also more than one way to solve a problem. This is a critical step in the problem-solving process and requires as much input as possible. As a general rule, those affected by the problem should be involved in this stage of the problem-solving process. In addition, any other person or group with knowledge and expertise relating to the problem and possible solutions should be asked for input during this phase. "For lack of guidance a nation falls, but many advisers make victory sure" (Prov. 11:14). This principle applies to business decisions as well as to national policy.

State the cost of each alternative. Every alternative has a unique cost factor—though not necessarily in terms of dollars and cents. One must consider the cost in time, energy, attitudes, and public opinion.

The cost factor plays an important role in determining which alternative will be selected.

Choose between alternatives. This stage of the problem-solving process frequently requires compromise. The most effective solution may not always be the best solution, once the cost factors have been considered. Problem-solving usually requires a great deal of give-and-take. What is viewed as a solution by one may not be by another. Therefore, the leader should consider the following:

- Does this solution violate biblical truth or principle?

- Does this solution meet the needs of those affected?

- Will people support the implementation of this solution?

- Will this solution create other problems?

- Will this solution help avoid problems in the future?

- Why should this solution be selected over the others?

Delegate action steps and begin implementation. Problem-solving requires change. Therefore, the problem isn't eliminated by making a decision, but only by implementing actions that bring about needed change.

Evaluate progress. As the implementation process begins, each action step should be monitored and evaluated to determine if the action is contributing to the solution of the problem. Frequently a solution that looks good on paper does not produce the desired results when implemented. When this occurs, corrections or new alternatives must be developed, implemented, and evaluated until the problem is eliminated and the desired result achieved.

According to numerous studies conducted by Management Training Systems, approximately ninety-five percent of the executive's time and work is spent dealing with and solving problems. A top executive in an international Christian organization recently told me, "It seems I spend all my time dealing with problems other people have been unable to solve. I have to admit I get awfully tired of it. If it weren't for our organization's exciting mission, I would have quit my job long ago."

The Christian leader's job is to serve the work-related needs of those under him. He can do this by helping them solve their problems. That's what Moses did. "The difficult cases they brought to Moses, but the simple ones they decided themselves" (Ex. 18:26). Moses became the problem-solver in difficult situations. His job was to serve others in this capacity.

The effective Christian leader or manager gives himself to helping those under him solve problems they are unable to overcome alone. Therefore, the leader must acquire effective decision-making and problem-solving skills.

Chapter Summary

Decision-making and problem-solving go hand in hand. The ability to make good decisions and solve problems effectively is among the most important skills a leader or manager can acquire.

For the Christian leader, knowing God's will is the foundation for decision-making and problem-solving. God has a specific plan for every individual and wants to make that plan a reality. In order to know God's plan, we must first be committed to putting God's will above our own. God not only promises to reveal His plan for us, but also to provide the resources and power needed to achieve it.

The Bible gives us guidelines for making decisions and solving problems. We must remember that even though God's plan for us is "good, pleasing, and perfect," we are not exempt from problems in carrying out those plans. Trials and problems come into our lives to help mature and perfect us (see James 1:2-4). Therefore, we should not have a negative attitude toward problems but should look at them as opportunities for personal growth.

Personal Application

Identify the issues or decisions you are currently facing.

Review the process for knowing God's will and make sure you are committed to doing God's will in each of the situations.

Apply the decision-making process and/or the problem-solving process to the most important issue on your list. Repeat the process until you have dealt with each item on the list.

CHAPTER 8

SUCCESSFUL COMMUNICATION SKILLS

As our rapid-paced, jet-propelled society rockets into the 21st century, it possesses the most sophisticated means of communication ever known to man. Modern electronic technology has made it possible for a man on the moon to converse with people on earth. And computer science is making it possible for man to converse with computers, which store and retrieve information in seconds that only a few short years ago took days and even weeks to process.

But even though man has developed highly sophisticated electronic communication machinery, he still has problems with personal, face-to-face communication. In fact, recent studies conducted by Management Training Systems with numerous organizations—both Christian and secular—indicated that poor communication was their number one leadership and management problem.

Defining Communication

What is communication? Most people admit they have problems communicating from time to time, but few take the time to define what they mean by "communication." Communication can be defined as *the process we go through to convey understanding from one person or group to another*. Unless understanding occurs, we have not communicated. Therefore, when people complain about poor communication, they are actually complaining about the lack of understanding and not about the lack of conversation, discussions, memos, or correspondence.

All too often we confuse the tools of communication with communication itself. Just because we have made the effort to communicate with someone, it doesn't guarantee that they'll automatically comprehend our message. Talking does not insure understanding, and written correspondence does not necessarily mean people understand the message.

I recently had an appointment with a seminary president and one of his administrators to discuss the management and leadership training needs of their students and alumni. The meeting was scheduled for two o'clock. At 2:15 the administrator still had not arrived. The president said, "I don't understand. I sent him a memo yesterday about this meeting."

We later found the administrator in the faculty lounge and discovered he had not picked up his interoffice mail for two days. The president assumed he had communicated with his administrator because he had sent a memo. Unfortunately, too often we assume that the tools of communication have produced understanding.

Jesus knew the importance of communication and He worked hard to make sure understanding occurred between Him and His disciples. After sharing several parables with them, Jesus asked, "Have you understood all these things?" (Matt. 13:51) Jesus recognized that unless understanding occurred, He was not communicating, regardless of how much preaching or lecturing He did.

The Importance of Communication

The building of the Tower of Babel (Gen. 11:1-9) vividly illustrates the important role communication plays in individual and organizational achievement. "Now the whole world had one language and a common speech" (v. 1). They had the ingredients of good communication as they organized to build "a city with a tower that reaches to the heavens" (v. 4).

God came down to observe the people and their project and said, "If as one people speaking the same language they have begun to do this, then nothing they plan to do will be impossible for them" (v. 6). God acknowledged that their effective communication system had unified them behind a common goal and motivated them to action.

Good communication is essential to the development of unity and motivation. Good communication is the basis for unlimited group innovation, creativity, and achievement.

God demonstrated the importance of communication by saying, "Come, let Us go down and confuse their language so they will not understand each other" (v. 7). Note here that communication is the development of understanding.

God also knew that in order to destroy productivity and shut down the project, He had to disrupt communication. Once their communication system was disrupted, the unity and motivation was destroyed and the project came to a standstill (v. 8).

This passage clearly illustrates the extremely important role communication plays in any organizational endeavor. Communication is the key to developing group unity, commitment, and motivation to work. It also provides the outlet for unlimited innovative and creative achievements. However, once understanding breaks down, unity, commitment, motivation, and group creativity are lost and the project fails.

We are all aware of the tremendous achievement of placing a man on the moon. Project Mercury, organized October 5, 1958, was designed to place the first American in outer space. This was accomplished just thirty months later on, May 5, 1961. Eight years later, July 16, 1969, we placed the first man on the moon. That event marked man's greatest technological achievement to date.

A space engineer who worked on the moon landing project told me, "Most people don't realize the magnitude of that endeavor. We had millions of people working on thousands of projects literally around the world during the life of that project in the 1960s. We knew good communication would be required to achieve our goal; therefore, we designed the simplest—yet most effective—communication system possible, and that was the key to our success."

God reveals and science confirms that communication plays one of the most vital roles in any organization's achievements. Therefore, it is imperative that the Christian leader, manager, or businessperson focus on acquiring effective communication skills.

The Communication Process

The definition of communication points out that a specific process is involved in the development of understanding. Therefore, becoming aware of this process and how each step is interrelated is one of the first requirements for improving communication.

Six steps are involved in the communication process. The first three steps must be taken by the person transmitting the message, and the last three by the one receiving the message.

The transmitter must:

- Develop a clear concept of the idea or feeling to be communicated

- Choose the right words and actions to convey the idea and/or feeling

- Become aware of the surrounding communication barriers and work at minimizing them

In addition to minimizing barriers, the receiver must:

- Absorb the transmitted information by listening to the words and observing the actions

- Translate the words and actions

- Develop correct ideas and feelings

Step One: Develop a clear concept of the idea or feeling to be communicated. In trying to get your ideas across to someone else, have you ever said, "I'm not really sure how to say this, but . . . "and then tried to explain yourself? Such a statement indicates you haven't formed a clear understanding of what you want to communicate. And if you don't really understand what you're trying to say, you can't expect others to understand you. Therefore, you have a responsibility to yourself and others to develop a clear concept of your ideas and feelings before attempting to pass them on to others.

Step Two: Choose the right words and actions to convey the idea and/or feeling. Understanding between individuals never occurs unless ideas and feelings are conveyed. Even though all of us are hesitant from time to time to state what we are thinking and feeling, we must keep in mind that withholding ideas and feelings is one of the greatest causes of misunderstanding.

I was conducting a management course for a hospital. One of the head nurses came to me during a lunch break and asked, "Are you aware of the problem you've caused?" She could tell by the surprised look on my face that I was unaware of any problem and continued. "I probably shouldn't be the one to tell you, but Martha, one of our new night supervisors, thinks you're trying to get her fired."

She explained that Martha felt I was using some of her personal mistakes as examples of poor supervision and had concluded I was trying to discredit her and get her fired.

I thanked the head nurse for the information, and after the class went to Martha's office to resolve the misunderstanding. I explained that I knew nothing about her personal supervisory experiences, had not used her as an example, and certainly had no reason to try to get her removed from her job. Within a few minutes, we had resolved the problem.

However, I explained to Martha she should have come to me with her thoughts and feelings. We would not have solved her problem had I not learned how she felt from someone else.

People are reluctant to share what they think and feel. Usually fear of rejection is predominant. Your thoughts and feelings represent you as a person. If you tell someone what you really think and how you actually feel, and they reject your ideas and feelings, they have rejected you.

In an effort to avoid rejection, most of us frequently withhold our true feelings and ideas, revealing only what we are sure is acceptable. As a result, we complain about communication problems, usually unaware that our unwillingness to share our ideas and feelings created the lack of understanding in the first place.

One day while I was shopping with my wife, Lorraine, she saw a dress in a store window. "Do you like that dress?" she asked.

I didn't really like it, but assuming she did and not wanting to hurt her feelings, I said yes. She later returned to town and bought it.

Not long ago I admitted I didn't like the dress. "You don't?" she said. "Well, I don't either. The only reason I bought it was because you said you liked it."

Our failure to state what we honestly thought and felt created misunderstanding and added an unwanted dress to my wife's wardrobe.

Ideas and feelings are communicated by words and actions. It has accurately been said, "Words do not have meaning, people have meanings for words." Therefore, when transmitting our ideas and feelings to others, we should make sure the words and actions used mean the same to the person receiving the message as they do to us.

Step Three: Become aware of the surrounding communication barriers and work at minimizing them. Communication is to an organization what blood is to the human body. When the blood supply is cut off from the hand, it becomes numb and the person loses its use. If the blood supply is not returned to the hand, eventually the flesh dies and gangrene develops. Left unattended, the gangrene will spread its poison to the rest of the body and bring death.

Communication represents the lifeblood of an organization. It transfers ideas, feelings, plans, and decisions into productive action. However, if barriers develop, cutting off the flow of communication to certain parts of the organization, these parts become ineffective and numb. Unless the communication barrier is removed, highly contagious organizational infections such as low morale, personality conflicts, negative attitudes of various kinds, and false assumptions will stifle that part of the organization's productivity. Left unchecked, these infections can eventually spread throughout the organization, reducing total productivity and eventually bringing organizational death. Therefore, it is extremely important to identify both individual and organizational barriers to communication and work at minimizing them and their impact on understanding.

It is impossible to eliminate all barriers to communication. However, most of them can be greatly minimized. A communication barrier can be defined as anything that inhibits or distorts efforts to develop understanding between individuals and groups.

During management seminars I frequently ask participants to list their most common communication barriers. Those most often stated are:

- Tuning people out and hearing only what we want to hear

- Allowing personal emotions to distort the information

- A lack of trust in the other's motives

- Noise or other distractions

- Differing value systems and perceptions

- Unwillingness to receive information that conflicts with pre-determined convictions or viewpoints

- Words that have several different meanings

- People's actions not corresponding with what is being said

While it is impossible to achieve complete and undistorted understanding between individuals, communication barriers can be minimized and misunderstandings greatly reduced by applying the following techniques:

- Whenever possible, use face-to-face communication

- Use direct, simple words (don't try to impress people with your grasp of the language)

- Solicit feedback from the listener

- Give your full attention to the speaker

- Never interrupt the speaker (who is not ready to listen to you until he has said what he is thinking and feeling)

- Encourage freedom of expression (agree to disagree; be willing to accept the other person's ideas and feelings as his or her own whether or not you agree with it)

Step Four: The receiver must absorb the transmitted information by listening to the words and observing the actions. The listener plays a very important role in the communication process. He must deal with the numerous communication barriers that tend to inhibit and distort the true idea or feeling, while at the same time observe the actions and listen to the words of the person sending the message. The importance of listening will be dealt with in detail later in the chapter.

Step Five: The receiver must translate the words and actions. The translation of words and actions into ideas and feelings is a very critical step in the development of understanding. A great deal of the original idea and feeling can be lost during this step in the communication process.

Step Six: The receiver must develop correct ideas and feelings. If the idea and feeling being sent in step one is the same idea and feeling being received in step six, understanding occurs and those involved have communicated effectively. On the other hand, if the idea and feeling in step six is different from that in step one, misunderstanding exists and communication has broken down.

The Role Listening Plays in the Communication Process

Management Training Systems has surveyed thousands of employees in an effort to determine the causes of poor communication. The survey results indicate that poor listening causes most misunderstanding. Studies reveal that the average person spends approximately 70 percent of his waking day in verbal communication, 45 percent of which is spent listening. In addition, research indicates that unless people have had specific training in listening, their efficiency in this skill is only 25 percent.

Much of the difficulty in listening is caused by the fact that the mind can listen faster than a person can talk. It is estimated that the average person can listen at a rate of 400 to 600 words a minute while most people can speak at only 200 to 300 words per minute. As a result, during conversations the mind tends to occupy itself with other things half of the time. This wandering of the mind causes the listener to miss a great deal of the ideas and feelings being presented.

How to Improve Listening Skills

Don't be afraid to ask questions for clarification. Failure to ask clarifying questions is one of the most common listener weaknesses. Many listeners are embarrassed to ask questions because they think it insinuates they were not paying attention in the first place. (Even if that were the case, it would be better to admit it during the conversation than after the fact.)

During my freshman and sophomore years in college, I worked part-time for a painter. One morning my boss took me to a house and told me how it was to be painted, including color combinations and trim work. Before leaving, he asked if I had any questions about the job. I didn't want my boss to think I hadn't been paying attention, so I said no.

Unfortunately, when my boss returned to check my work, he learned I hadn't understood the instructions. I had used the wrong color on the trim and one of the interior walls. As a result, most of the work had to be done over. Had I been willing to ask questions for clarification, the mistake could easily have been avoided.

Don't start formulating your response while the speaker is still talking. Most of us are poor listeners simply because we would rather talk than listen. We're thinking about what we're going to say while the speaker is still talking. This causes lack of concentration and contributes greatly to misunderstanding.

Avoid premature or false assumptions about what the speaker is going to say. If we think we know what a person is going to say, what we assume will be said is frequently what we hear—whether it is said or not. Listeners sometimes interrupt the speaker with, "I know what you're thinking," or "I know what you're going to say." This demonstrates they have made premature, possibly false, assumptions about the speaker's ideas and feelings. Such assumptions make it difficult to develop an understanding of the true message being presented.

Several years ago I worked for a boss who regularly interrupted me to say he knew what I was about to say or what I was thinking. As a result, he heard only what he wanted to hear, which frequently was not what I was saying at all. He was very difficult to work with—and for—because he was a poor listener. Yet he prided himself on what he thought was the ability to "understand where you are coming from." However, more often than not, this resulted in misunderstandings, and led eventually to my resignation.

Avoid interrupting the speaker. Even apart from falsely assuming we know what's about to be said, we may tend to interrupt others unwisely. We forget that there is "a time to be silent and a time to speak" (Ecc. 3:7). This is an important communication principle. Certainly a time to keep silent is while the other person is sharing his ideas and feelings. Several things happen to the flow of understanding when a speaker is interrupted.

1. The flow and development of the speaker's complete message is disrupted, making it more difficult to understand the details of what is being said.

2. The speaker has difficulty listening to your statements because he is still thinking about his own.

3. The listener has demonstrated he feels what he has to say is more important than the speaker's thoughts.

4. The listener has demonstrated he has made an assumption concerning the rest of the speaker's comments.

Obviously, all of these factors contribute significantly to misunderstanding. Therefore, every time you or someone else involved in the conversation interrupts the speaker, you can be sure there is a great deal of potential for misunderstanding.

Work at minimizing the "filtering effect" of your prejudices. All of us have prejudices that filter and dilute our understanding. For example, if we are prejudiced toward people we consider "hippies," as we listen to them our prejudices distort what they say, creating misunderstanding. Therefore, we should become aware of our prejudices toward various people and topics, and when dealing with them, ask clarifying questions to help insure understanding.

Listen for the ideas and feelings behind the words being spoken. Words are only a vehicle by which ideas and feelings are transported. Studies indicate that in some situations as little as 7 percent of the complete message is communicated in the words spoken. The remaining

93 percent is transmitted through tone of voice or some nonverbal action or expression (see fig. 9). For understanding to occur, the listener must train himself to listen for the ideas and feelings being communicated "behind" the words.

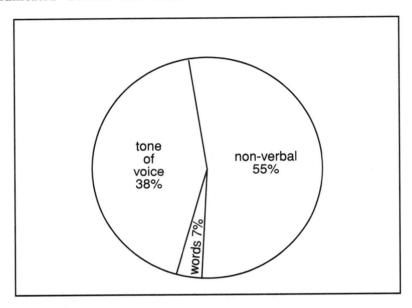

Figure 9. This diagram shows how a complete message may be transmitted. Surprisingly, what we say may not be nearly as important as the way we say it.

We must become "perceptive listeners," learning to hear more than the words being spoken. Paul demonstrated his perceptive listening ability when he said, "Men of Athens! I see that in every way you are very religious" (Acts 17:22). Paul didn't learn this simply by listening to the words of their philosophers. He also observed their actions (v. 23).

Perceptive listening, then, focuses on listening for the meaning in nonverbal actions and tone of voice because that is what produces 93 percent of the message. Mark 8:13-21 provides a classic example of Jesus' disciples failing to use perceptive listening, and as a result, misunderstanding what Jesus was saying.

Following the feeding of the 4,000, Jesus and His disciples got in a boat and started across the Sea of Galilee on their way to Bethsaida. During the trip Jesus told the disciples to avoid the leaven of the Pharisees. The disciples discussed this among themselves and decided He was reprimanding them for failing to bring along bread. Overhearing their conversation, Jesus confronted them. "Why are you talking about having no bread? Do you still not see or understand?" (v. 17)

The disciples had been poor listeners for several reasons. First, they were listening only to the words being spoken and not to the ideas and feelings behind the words. They were not perceptive listeners. Second, they failed to ask clarifying questions. Instead, they discussed among themselves what Jesus may have meant. As a result, they totally misunderstood the point of Jesus' admonition.

Jesus wasn't concerned with the lack of bread for a meal. He had just fed 4,000 men with seven loaves. He was speaking about the sin and lack of faith of the Pharisees as evidenced by His conversation with them prior to leaving in the boat (see vv. 11-12).

This passage provides a classic case study in poor listening. It illustrates what happens when we listen only to the speaker's words and fail to perceive his meaning. It also points out how reluctant people are to ask questions for clarification, and what happens when they don't. However, Jesus was an excellent communicator and perceived that they were confused about what He was saying. Therefore, He clarified His statement.

Attitudes Needed for Perceptive Listening

The listener must want to hear the speaker. Many people are poor listeners simply because they are not interested in what the speaker has to say. The listener must keep in mind that the speaker feels what he is saying is important and needs to be presented or he wouldn't be talking. Therefore, the listener must develop an attitude of wanting to hear what is being said.

Eye contact is the best way of communicating that you want to hear the speaker. It also helps the listener keep his attention on what is being said and how it is being presented. It is impossible to use perceptive listening without eye contact, since much of the message is transmitted nonverbally and is understood through observation.

The listener must be willing to accept the ideas and feelings of the speaker. This does not mean one has to agree with what the speaker says and thinks. However, the listener must be willing to let the speaker have his own views, opinions, ideas and feelings.

Keep in mind that a person's ideas and feelings represent his real self. If the listener is not willing to let the speaker have his own ideas and feelings, he is actually communicating: "I am not willing to let you be yourself; I am rejecting you." Therefore, as stated earlier, the listener must convey the attitude: "I respect your right to have these ideas and feelings, even though I may not agree with them."

This is an extremely important attitude to convey when dealing with controversial issues that could lead to conflict. Communicating you are willing to recognize the speaker's right to his views helps him avoid becoming defensive and unwilling to tell you what he really thinks and feels. The listener should be ever mindful of the Scripture that says, "A man who lacks judgment derides his neighbor, but a man of understanding holds his tongue"(Prov. 11:12).

Focus on Keeping Communication Simple

Paul wrote to the Corinthians, "Dear brothers, even when I first came to you I didn't use lofty words and brilliant ideas to tell you God's message" (1 Cor. 2:1, TLB). Corinth was an industrialized metropolis that boasted being one of the largest centers of trade and culture in the Roman Empire. However, Paul reminded the people that even though they lived in a center of education and culture, he didn't try to impress them with his big words. Paul was a good communicator because of his ability to present great truths in simple, easy-to-understand language. This is an important key to good communication.

Unfortunately, the trend today is toward saturating our messages with numerous nondescript, multisyllabic words that carry little meaning. My daughter, who is a freshman in college, recently came home from an introductory communication course very frustrated with the instructor. "My teacher has a doctorate in communication, but most of us can't understand him because he uses big words trying to impress us with how smart he is," she said. She tossed me her notes from that day's class and said, "Here, read this definition of memory he gave us today."

I picked up her notes and read, "As relating to learning, memory is the storage and retrieval of the relatively stable potential for subsequent occurrence of the response."

"Now I ask you," my daughter said, "what in the world does that mean?" I had to admit there should be a simpler way to define memory.

Some of the greatest statements ever made were the simplest. The Lord's Prayer contains 56 words. The Gettysburg Address has 267 words. The Declaration of Independence contains 1,322 words. By contrast, a recent government regulation on the sale of cabbage contains 26,901 words. The trend toward wordiness is one major cause of communication problems.

The Formula for Developing Understanding

Developing understanding is relatively easy, provided the individuals involved keep communication simple and honestly share their ideas, feelings, and attitudes. Understanding is easily achieved when the following formula is used:

When _____ (occurs), I feel
_____ (state the way you feel),
because _____ (state why you
feel that way).

This communication formula causes the speaker to state exactly what he thinks and feels and why. Unless that information is shared, the listener has a great deal of difficulty determining what is really being said.

Chapter Summary

When God first called Moses to lead the Children of Israel out of Egypt, Moses replied, "O Lord, I have never been eloquent . . . I am slow of speech and tongue" (Ex. 4:10). When God called Jeremiah to be a prophet to the nation of Israel, Jeremiah said, "Ah, Sovereign Lord...I do not know how to speak" (Jer. 1:6). Feeling inadequate as a communicator is an experience common to most of us, at least at times.

However, every good leader is a good communicator. He has the ability to convey understanding to others. Good communication develops and maintains unity, commitment, and motivation in achieving a goal. In fact, communication is the lifeblood of an organization; without it the group dies.

Communication begins with the speaker making sure he clearly understands what he wants to communicate. He must be careful to choose the proper words and actions to transmit his message simply and correctly.

Both speaker and listener must become aware of the numerous communication barriers that hamper understanding and work to minimize their impact on the communication process.

The listener plays a vital role in effective communication. He must concentrate to hear what is actually said. The listener must learn to listen to the meaning behind the words being spoken because 93 percent of the message is communicated in the tone of voice and through various nonverbal actions.

The good communicator speaks accurately and listens properly. He states clearly and simply what he thinks and feels and then listens effectively to the thoughts and feelings of others.

Personal Application

Identify the people closest to you in a working relationship.

What are the communication barriers that exist between you and these people?

What can be done to minimize these barriers?

Review the communication process outlined in this chapter and determine what steps you should work at improving. Make this a special project in the days ahead until good communication becomes a habit.

Review the section on listening, and determine where your listening skills need improving. Make a project out of becoming a perceptive listener.

CHAPTER 9

WHEN AND HOW TO DELEGATE

B
ud Walters has owned and operated his own construction company for the past thirty-seven years. Recently his son Jerry came
to my office and during our conversation said, "Myron, I'm
considering leaving my dad's company and going to work somewhere
else." When I asked why, Jerry continued, "I have watched my dad
build this business from nothing. However, now the business is running him instead of him running the business."

"What's the problem?" I asked, not wanting to sound too nosy.

"Well," he said, "Dad never learned to delegate responsibility. As
the company has grown, he has tried to keep on top of every aspect of
the operation. I've tried to get him to slow down and let me help more
with some of the details, but he seems to think things can't run without him." He shook his head. "I'm afraid that the business is going to
be the death of him yet."

Mike Simpson, an assistant pastor of a large church on the East
Coast told me during a management seminar, "I don't understand my
boss (the senior pastor). He acts as if he's the only one who can do
anything in the church. He has to be on all the committees—in fact,
they all meet in his office—and nothing can be done without his
approval." He concluded, "It really gets frustrating because we have

lots of people willing to do things, yet he runs around spinning his wheels trying to do it all."

As a management consultant, I have listened to countless employees complain about their boss' inability to delegate. A person may be in a leadership position, but if he isn't willing to delegate, he isn't a leader at all—he is the "hired hand." Unfortunately, many of our "full-time Christian workers" in leadership positions of Christian organizations never learn to become full-time Christian managers.

Defining Delegation

Delegation consists of transferring authority, responsibility, and accountability from one person or group to another. In most cases, it involves moving authority from a higher level in an organization to a lower one. Delegation is the process by which decentralization of organizational power occurs. Decentralization involves the dispersion of authority and responsibility from the top downward through the organization, allowing more people to become involved in the decision-making processes.

A Biblical Case Study on Delegation

Exodus 18:13-26 provides an excellent case study on delegation. The setting involves Moses' leadership of the Children of Israel on their way to Canaan.

Moses resembled many present-day Christian leaders. He was a spiritual man and provided strong spiritual leadership. However, he lacked the management skills needed to accomplish the job God had called him to do.

The passage begins by describing a typical day in Moses' life as the leader of the people. "The next day Moses took his seat to serve as judge for the people, and they stood around him from morning till evening" (v. 13). This is a pathetic scene. The people probably stood in long lines—apparently all day long—waiting to get a decision out of Moses. This bottleneck of authority at the head of the nation must have greatly reduced their forward progress as they traveled.

Moses' father-in-law, Jethro, observed the situation and asked, "What is this you are doing for the people?" (v. 14) Notice that Moses was working hard doing things for the people. Jethro also asked, "Why do you alone sit as judge, while all these people stand around you from morning till evening?" (v. 14)

Jethro asked very probing questions. In answering them, Moses revealed his philosophy of leadership and management. He declared that as the spiritual leader he was in a better position to answer the questions correctly and make the proper decisions. "I decide between the parties and inform them of God's decrees and laws" (v. 16).

Notice Jethro's response, "What you are doing is not good" (v. 17). Can you believe that? The audacity of Jethro! Moses had carefully explained to this "outsider" that he was making all the decisions because, as the spiritual leader, he was in a better position to teach them about God and to know what God really wanted done.

Notice Jethro's further comments: "You and these people who come to you will only wear yourselves out. The work is too heavy for you; you cannot handle it alone" (v. 18). Here Jethro points out the results when leaders fail to delegate decision-making power to others and decentralize authority. The people, as well as the leader, become worn out. The people become frustrated because of how long they have to wait for results. The leader is worn out and exhausted from making all the decisions for the people and organization.

Over the past several years I have observed that same scene in numerous churches and other Christian organizations. The people are worn out waiting for something to happen as a result of their input or request, and the leadership is exhausted from trying to make all the right decisions themselves.

Jethro, however, explained that Moses should divide up the decision-making power and responsibility and delegate it to trustworthy men. "Have them serve as judges for people at all times, but have them bring every difficult case to you; the simple cases they can decide themselves. That will make your load lighter, because they will share it with you" (v. 22).

Many leaders and managers try to use this part of the passage to justify their lack of delegation by saying, "If I had competent, trustworthy people to put in authority, I would do it in a minute. But I don't have people with the experience needed for the job."

The people to whom Moses delegated authority didn't have the experience either. They had not held that job back in Egypt. The only thing on their resumes was making bricks. Therefore, the word *trustworthy* in this passage cannot mean Moses picked people with lots of experience in leadership and decision-making. It simply means he picked people who were honest in character.

Moses could have taken his father-in-law outside the camp and said, "Listen, Pop, you may do things that way where you came from, but we don't do it that way here." No, he was willing to let an "outsider" teach him how to improve his leadership ability.

Moses recognized and admitted he had a problem and was willing to change, even if it meant giving some authority for decisions to others. The people Moses picked to help him lead "served as judges for the people at all times. The difficult cases they brought to Moses, but the simple ones they decided themselves" (v. 26).

Advantages of Effective Delegation

This passage points out several advantages of delegation:

Delegation makes the manager's job easier. Like Moses, many modern Christian leaders are wearing themselves out trying to cope with the many problems and pressures of running a Christian organization. Delegation helps free the leader, giving him the time and energy to deal with most important aspects of management and leadership.

Delegation increases productivity. Delegation not only makes it possible for the leader to be more productive, but it increases the efficiency of the entire organization. Needed decisions can be made faster, and as a result, the needs are met more quickly.

Delegation develops additional leadership. Most Christian organizations do not have much depth when it comes to leadership. Managers do not have time to develop the leadership of other people because they are too busy running the organization. As a result, the manager feels there isn't anyone else trained to assist in the leadership. Delegation develops leadership ability. It gives people decision-making and problem-solving experience and helps prepare them for greater responsibility.

One leader of a large international Christian organization recently told me, "The only thing keeping us from growing as an organization is our lack of trained leaders." He also admitted management's unwillingness to delegate had created their leadership shortage.

The early church experienced rapid growth because its leadership was willing to delegate. At one point, the 12 Apostles were not adequately meeting the needs of all the people because of the growth. What did they do? They delegated authority to others to meet the needs instead of trying to do everything themselves. This developed additional leaders and also gave the apostles time for their own spiritual growth. The result: "So the word of God spread. The number of disciples in Jerusalem increased rapidly" (Acts 6:7).

Delegation gives the Christian leader more time for his personal spiritual development. This passage in Acts (6:1-7) illustrates one reason for delegating in Christian organizations. Some Christian leaders are so busy with the day-to-day details of managing the organization that they don't take time to find out what God is doing and wants to do through them.

The 12 Apostles realized they couldn't allow themselves to get caught in the trap of handling more and more responsibility. To do so would rob them of their much-needed time with God in prayer and the study of His Word. Therefore, they used delegation to insure they had plenty of time to spend with God. The Christian leader bogged down with the routine details of management and leadership may be working in a Christian organization, but he probably isn't accomplishing the plans God has for him. To do God's will, the leader must spend enough time with God to find out what His will is.

The Christian leader's first responsibility is to God. Therefore, he must make sure he spends the necessary time with God required to manage God's work. Delegation provides that time.

Delegation stimulates employee creativity. Delegation makes the employee feel a part of the organizational team. Jim Kegin, a friend of mine, used to be salesman for a meat-processing firm in Oklahoma. One day Jim's boss said to him, "I've decided to let you set your prices when you sell to our customers." He explained to Jim how much it would cost per pound to process the meat Jim was selling. He said the company would like to maintain a 20 percent margin of profit if possible. However, Jim could set a price at which he felt he could sell the meat.

The added responsibility of pricing the meat for the customer made Jim more aware of the importance of his role with the company. He began working harder to make a profit. He also began thinking about how he could develop new markets. Within six months he had not only doubled his sales, but had also increased the firm's margin of profit. By delegating decision-making power and responsibility, Jim's boss motivated him to become more creative in his work. In addition, it freed up Jim's boss to work on other management needs.

Delegation demonstrates trust and confidence in employee ability. Al Truesdale used to work as a small-business tax specialist for the Internal Revenue Service. One day he told me he was quitting his job. I jokingly asked him if he was getting tired of chasing tax evaders. He said, "No, but I'm sure getting tired of working for a boss who doesn't trust his people to do the job they were hired to do. He only lets me do the simple and routine jobs. Every time a big case comes along, he does it himself or gives it to the assistant manager."

Al had concluded his boss didn't trust his ability because he wouldn't delegate important projects to him. Al started his own tax consulting business and currently handles some of the largest accounts in the area. His manager not only lost a good employee, but he had been wasting his time doing work that Al could have done.

Delegation stimulates employee motivation and commitment to the organization. J. Paul Getty believed in delegation. He was willing to trust people and give them decision-making power. As a result, he recruited some of the best employees in the business.

When Getty first started in the oil business, he was unable to compete with the salaries and fringe benefits of his larger competitors. However, he always had some of the best workers in the oil fields. One day a driller from another company came to Getty and asked for a job. "Why do you want to work for me?" Getty asked. "I can't begin to pay you what you're making now. Besides, my men have to drive back and forth to town each day and stay in a rented room they pay for themselves, while your boss furnishes living quarters on the job."

The driller grinned at Getty and said, "But your men tell me you come to them for advice and let them get involved in deciding how the well will be drilled." He went on, "I'd be glad to take less money to work for a boss like that."

Most employees say the same thing. When the manager delegates authority and responsibility to them, they become loyal workers with a commitment to the organization.

Every Manager Needs to Delegate More

I have never met a manager who was delegating everything he should. The diagram in figure 10 explains why. The manager is

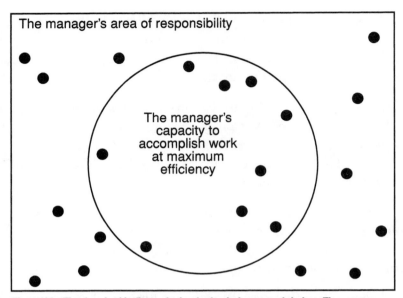

Figure 10. The dots in this figure depict the leader's personal duties. The square represents his total area of responsibility and the circle represents his capacity to get work done at maximum efficiency. Notice that his area of responsibility is greater that his ability to do all of the tasks at maximum efficiency.

responsible for more than he can handle efficiently. This does not mean he doesn't get his work done. He generally does—eventually. However, because of the scope of his responsibilities, some of his duties and activities are not accomplished quickly. Some tasks do not get his full attention simply because he does not have enough time and energy. Therefore, the manager frequently finds himself trying to stretch his capacity to encompass all of the many activities he needs to accomplish.

Managers facing this dilemma are generally easily identified. They skip coffee breaks and lunch hours to finish up a project. They arrive first to work and leave last. They return to the office on weekends to tie up loose ends. Unfortunately, many of their peers mistakenly refer to them as "good company people" and greatly admire their loyalty and commitment to their work. Occasionally some of their bosses call them the backbone of the organization, and almost always their spouses call them things that shouldn't be put in print. However, in reality they are leaders and managers who have not yet learned to delegate responsibility.

As a management consultant, I have little sympathy for such managers. They complain about their heavy schedules and not having enough time to get everything done. I have never met a manager who, once he understood and used delegation properly, was still so overworked he had to put in sixty hours a week just to keep up. (If he is putting in that much time, it is because he wants to—not because he needs to.) Unfortunately, I have met countless managers who had to work overtime every day and on weekends simply because they had not learned how to delegate. Like Moses, they were wearing themselves out doing jobs that could and should have been done by others.

The Delegation Process

Step One: Recognize the limits of your capacity. Most managers do not delegate their decision-making power to others until they realize they are overextended. Moses didn't delegate authority to others until he became aware of the need. Getting leaders and managers to admit they need to delegate is frequently more difficult than it sounds. Most leaders hate to admit they should get others involved in assisting them with part of their responsibilities.

Wanda Hinsley is the personnel director for an electronics firm. She is a hard worker and has lots of enthusiasm for the company. As a result, over the years she has taken on more and more projects and responsibilities, including public relations projects, training functions, office interior decorating projects, overseeing the plant's internal communications network, keeping an eye on the internal mail system, and overseeing the administrative secretarial pool.

Since the Hinsleys are our next-door neighbors, I frequently chat with Wanda concerning her job and the company's various activities. For the past few years I have watched her steadily become overextended at work. Recently while talking with me over the backyard fence, she described a new project for which she had volunteered.

When I asked her how she intended to find time for the job, she smiled and said, "Oh, I'll manage to squeeze it in somewhere."

Wanda, like many other leaders, has allowed her enthusiasm for her work to catch her in an activity trap. Her responsibilities are extended far beyond her capacity to get work done efficiently. Yet she continues to take on more work. When others suggest she should delegate responsibility instead of taking on new projects, she laughs and argues that she can handle it. Some would excuse her by saying she is "just a workaholic." The truth is, a once-good manager has failed to recognize the limits of her capacity and therefore does not see the need to delegate to others.

Managers should not wait until they have reached their capacity to begin delegating. Delegation gives employees an opportunity to develop leadership skills, learn how to solve problems, and use their creativity. It also gives the manager more time to focus on the major areas of importance. Therefore, the manager should constantly work at delegating projects whether he is overextended or not.

Step Two: Determine the purpose of the delegation. Delegation serves many purposes. It can be used to give the manager more time for other activities, to train employees as leaders, to show recognition, and to broaden employees' technical skills. Therefore, the manager should determine why he is delegating, because that will greatly influence what is delegated and who gets the assignment.

For example, if the manager wants to use delegation to begin training more leaders, he would pick projects involving problem-solving, decision-making, and planning—not routine tasks already understood by the employee.

Never use delegated jobs to keep people busy. Busywork accomplishes nothing and communicates that the manager is more interested in activity than productivity. In addition, busywork is seen by employees as punishment and lowers their morale. It shows employees that the leader is not a good manager because he is unable to plan and organize properly. Busywork is the manager's effort to look good in the eyes of his boss at the employees' expense.

Step Three: Select the projects or activities to be delegated. Once the manager determines why he needs to delegate, next he must identify the projects and activities to be assigned. Needless to say, the purpose will greatly influence which activities are selected. The manager should not just pick the first activity that comes to mind; he should make sure it is the one best suited to accomplish the purpose.

Step Four: Select the person or people to be given the assignment. In making this selection, the leader or manager should answer the following questions:

- Which employee is best suited for the job in terms of experience and training?

- Is one employee more interested in the activity than others?

- Will the individual have enough time to accomplish the added responsibility in addition to his regular duties?

- When will the employee be available to begin?

- Will the employee selected need special assistance or training?

Matching the right people with the right assignment is the key to successful delegation, and a skill too few managers have mastered. Jethro told Moses, "Select capable men from all the people—men who fear God, trustworthy men who hate dishonest gain" (Ex. 18:21). Similarly, Nehemiah said, "I put in charge of Jerusalem my brother Hanani, along with Hananiah the commander of the citadel, because he was a man of integrity and feared God more than most men do"(Neh. 7:2). These verses point out the importance of picking the right person for the job. Failure to do so can mean failure of the project being delegated.

Step Five: Meet with the employee selected for the project and explain all instructions, requirements, and other important factors associ-

ated with the assignment. Good communication is an important part of the delegation process. When assigning the project, make sure the following points are understood by the employee:

- When the assignment begins

- All instructions concerning how the project must be done

- What decision-making power the employee has in doing the job

- What resources are available to assist him (such as people, equipment, supplies)

- Any special procedures involved in accomplishing the task

- Who the employee answers to and where he goes for help

- The purpose of the project, its importance, and where it fits in the overall scheme of other projects and activities

- How the employee's performance will be evaluated

Misunderstanding by the employee on any one of the above points can lead to problems—or even failure. Therefore, this is an extremely important step in the delegation process. Be willing to take as much time as needed to insure that the employee understands each point. Also, encourage him to come to you or other appropriate individuals any time he has a question.

Covering these points helps give the employee security in his ability to do the job correctly and motivates him to assume other assignments as needed. I learned this the hard way while working as a manager in private industry. One day I asked for a volunteer to work on an important assignment. One of my best employees agreed to take on the project. I met with her and explained it was a very important job that had to be completed before the end of the day. However, I failed to tell her the location of some of the material needed to do the work. After giving her the assignment, I left the office. When I returned late in the afternoon, she was almost in tears.

She had been unable to find the supplies and therefore could not complete the project. At first I was extremely upset with her. However, I quickly realized it was my fault, not hers. My failure to give her all the information needed caused the project to be late, which resulted in my boss being quite upset with me. However, the greatest tragedy was that one of my best employees became reluctant to volunteer for special projects because of my failure to explain all of the information needed to do the job.

Step Six: Maintain open communication with the employee while he works on the project. Some managers make the mistake of delegating a project, but not maintaining communication with the employee while he or she is doing the work. Maintaining regular communication with the employee helps avoid unforeseen problems and also lets the employee know you are interested and available to meet work-related needs.

Elements of Successful Delegation

There are three important elements of delegation—responsibility, authority, and accountability. Responsibility represents the activity to be performed. When delegating responsibility, make sure the employee knows exactly what is to be done. Authority represents the decision-making power needed to achieve the assigned responsibility. Accountability is the obligation to perform the responsibility and exercise authority in terms of established performance standards.

In order for managerial delegation to be successful, the employee must know what the responsibilities are, how much authority he has to make decisions needed to accomplish the assigned task, and that he will be held accountable for his actions.

The manager should never assign responsibility without giving the authority needed to do the job. Several years ago I was working as a personnel director and given the responsibility of writing personnel policies and procedures for the corporation. However, I soon learned I did not have authority to determine how they were written. Much to my surprise, when my boss returned the first policy I wrote, it had been completely rewritten. I soon learned to find out exactly how he wanted the policy to read and then recopy his statements.

It dawned on me that I was nothing more than a glorified secretary. I lost interest in my job and within a few months resigned and went to work for a boss who was willing to delegate authority with responsibility.

How to Delegate without Losing Control

Many managers are reluctant to delegate because they feel it causes them to lose control over results. A manager once told me, "Every time I delegate an important project I have trouble sleeping at night until it is done. I'm afraid it won't be done right—and after all, I am accountable."

Failure to specify the boundary lines of authority creates most control problems in delegation. Don Jamison, a realtor and excellent instructor, was hired by a Midwestern university's department of continuing education to enroll students and teach real estate classes on a part-time basis. Don was an energetic individual and within a few days had completely revised the program. He deleted some of the classes and added others he felt would sell better. In addition, he made arrangements to offer real estate classes in communities that had not been on the original schedule.

The continuing education department had spent a considerable amount of time and effort developing the schedule and getting courses approved, and the director was extremely upset when he discovered what Don had done. So much so that he fired Don.

Later I discussed the situation with the director. He said, "Don is a good realtor and fine instructor, but he made some inexcusable mistakes." I asked if anyone had informed Don when he was hired what his role was to be and how much authority he would have. The director said, "Well, I suppose it was partly our fault for not explaining that to him specifically." In reality, most of the blame belonged to the director. All of the mistakes could have been avoided if he had clearly communicated to Don what the boundary lines of his authority were.

Boundary lines of authority allow the manager to anticipate the decisions and actions of his subordinates. Suppose you own a lumber business and I work as your supervisor in the yard. I have been a good supervisor for several years and you realize you need to delegate more to me. You call me into your office and say, "Myron, I've decided to let you start hiring the new employees who will work for you in the yard." I thank you, knowing that all along I could have done a better job than you have been doing. The following Monday morning I start interviewing prospective employees.

I interview one man who has twelve years of experience working in lumberyards in Oregon, but he wants too much money. He also wants all Saturdays off. We work Saturday mornings, but I remember you have given me authority to make the decision, so I hire him at $2 an hour more than other employees at the same level and tell him he can have Saturdays off.

How will you respond? That's right, you will be extremely upset and probably decide you can't trust me with the authority to make decisions. However, my mistake was your fault. You should have told me how much I could pay the employees, what the working hours had to be, and any other special requirements such as skills or physical strength. I would still have had the authority to hire the employees. However, both of us would have understood the limitations, as illustrated in figure 11.

Authority boundaries protect both the manager and subordinate by identifying where decision-making power ends and recommendations begin. It is important to understand that on both sides of the

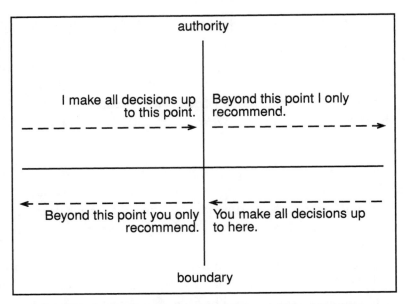

Figure 11. This diagram illustrates how boundaries work in the delegation process. Every time decision-making power is delegated, the authority boundaries should be clarified.

authority boundary, decisions are made in conjunction with input from others. Both the manager and the subordinate should continue to seek such input even though they individually have the responsibility to make the final decision.

Authority boundaries help eliminate confusion as to who is responsible for making the decision on any given activity or project. This makes it easier to build in accountability for action and for results. Boundaries serve to clarify limits of authority and help both the leader and subordinate feel more secure in their roles. The leader doesn't have to worry that subordinates will make surprise decisions outside guidelines or policy. On the other hand, the subordinate doesn't have to worry about overstepping his authority when making decisions.

Authority boundaries also help the manager avoid the trap of delegating a project to an employee and then discovering the employee has delegated it back to him. Many employees feel insecure with decision-making responsibility. They delegate the assignment back to the boss by continually asking what should be done about this or that matter related to the project. The manager can easily find himself answering such questions and ultimately making the decisions for the subordinate. However, if authority boundaries have been clearly identified, the manager can simply remind the employee it is his responsibility to make the decision within given guidelines.

Finally, it should be pointed out that as the subordinate develops his problem-solving and decision-making ability, the authority boundary can—and should—be extended.

Why Managers Fail to Delegate

Over the past several years I have heard numerous reasons and excuses from managers as to why they don't delegate. Here are the three most common:

- The job will not be done the way I would do it.

- My subordinates lack the necessary training to perform the job.

- I enjoy doing the work, and therefore do not want to delegate.

The job will not be done the way I would do it. This is the most common excuse for not delegating. When a manager feels a subordinate would not do the job the way he would do it, he is right. No two people do things exactly the same way. Unfortunately, the manager who uses this excuse is setting himself up as the performance model by which everything is to be evaluated. He is also limiting people in what they can accomplish. If he would delegate, he would soon learn that not only would his subordinate do the job differently, but also he would often do it better. As long as the manager avoids delegating, he is making sure the organization never accomplishes more than he personally can plan, think, create, and produce.

My subordinates lack the necessary training to perform the job. This is an amusing excuse because the leader is admitting his own failure as a manager and developer of people. Delegation is one of the most effective and least expensive training tools available to a manager. The manager who says he cannot delegate because his people lack training is admitting he should delegate in order to train them.

I enjoy doing the work, and therefore do not want to delegate. This is a common problem among leaders and managers, especially among those promoted from within the organization. More than likely, at one time they did the job some subordinates should be doing. Since people tend to gravitate to the familiar, it is easy for the manager to have difficulty letting go of his former responsibilities. This is generally a bigger problem for newly promoted managers than for those in the position for some time.

God Set the Example for Delegation

Psalm 8:3-6 describes God's philosophy and attitude toward delegation. "When I look up into the night skies and see the work of Your fingers—the moon and the stars You have made—I cannot understand how You can bother with mere puny man, to pay any attention to him! And yet You have made him only a little lower than the angels, and placed a crown of glory and honor upon his head. You have put him in charge of everything You made; everything is put under his authority", (TLB).

What an example for the Christian leader to follow! Here we have a description of God creating the universe and then, after finishing His wonderfully perfect work, putting man in charge of it. What a display of trust, confidence, and love. If God is willing to put us in charge of what He has so perfectly made, how much more should the Christian leader be willing to delegate authority and responsibility to those under him?

Chapter Summary

Delegation can be defined as the process of transferring authority, responsibility, and accountability from one person or group to another. Exodus 18:13-26 provides an excellent case study concerning why delegation is needed and what is involved.

Delegation makes the leader's job easier and at the same time helps increase individual and group productivity. It is an excellent training tool and helps develop strong leaders within the group. It also gives the Christian leader more time for his personal spiritual development.

Every manager needs to work at delegating more. He needs to learn to use delegation effectively, making sure he understands the value of delegation and then picks the right people for the job.

Many managers are afraid to delegate because they feel they lose control of results. This fear can be eliminated easily by identifying the boundary lines of authority as it is delegated to a subordinate.

The manager should keep in mind that unless he learns to delegate effectively, he is nothing more than a hired hand—a full-time Christian worker holding a leadership position that should be filled by a full-time Christian manager.

Personal Application

Study figure 10 and identify the current activities within your area of responsibility that are outside your capacity to pursue at maximum efficiency.

Next, review the delegation process and begin using it to delegate those activities identified above.

In delegating each project, make sure the authority boundaries are clearly identified.

Keep a record of the results from delegation.

CHAPTER 10

TIME MANAGEMENT

Will Rogers used to say, "It's not so much what you do each day—it's what you get done that counts." Paul emphasized this same point by writing, "Be very careful, then, how you live—not as unwise but as wise, making the most of every opportunity, because the days are evil" (Eph. 5:15-16). "Be wise in the way you act toward outsiders; make the most of every opportunity" (Col. 4:5).

Aristotle Onassis, the multimillionaire business tycoon who made fortunes in the shipping business, was once asked to share his secret of success. He replied, "I have learned the value and importance of time; therefore, I work two additional hours each day and in that way, I gain the equivalent of one additional month each year."

Dawson Trotman, the founder and first president of The Navigators, once said, "The greatest time wasted is the time getting started."

The above quotes all have one thing in common—they stress the value and importance of time. Both God and man, Christian leader and secular businessperson, agree that time is to be used and not wasted.

What Is Time?

Not long ago I was reviewing my pocket calendar, checking what I had done each day during the previous several weeks. As I turned the pages I suddenly realized I was reviewing the major actions and events of my life. I had a new awareness that *time is the passing of life.* As I thought about that, time took on new meaning and importance. I realized that people who have problems managing their time actually have problems managing their lives.

Time is your most valuable resource. Time is unique, because unlike other resources, it cannot be stored or saved. We frequently hear people say, "I need to save time." But time cannot be saved or stored up for later use—you must use it as you receive it. What you are and what you possess is the result of how you have used the time allotted to you. Therefore, one can look at your possessions and listen to your conversations and determine how you have apportioned your time.

All of us have the same amount of time. Time does not discriminate. All of us have the same 60 minutes in an hour, 24 hours in a day, 7 days in a week, and 52 weeks in a year. The difference is in the way we use the time we have.

Therefore, the secret to time management is not in learning how to save time or get more out of it. The secret is in knowing how to use wisely the 60 minutes in every hour.

In part, the secret is to be industrious, as the Bible so colorfully says:

Take a lesson from the ants, you lazy fellow. Learn from their ways and be wise! For though they have no king to make them work, yet they labor hard all summer, gathering food for the winter. But you—all you do is sleep. When will you wake up?

"Let me sleep a little longer!"

Sure, just a little more! And as you sleep, poverty creeps upon you like a robber and destroys you; want attacks you in full armor (Prov. 6:6-11, TLB).

Time Robbers

"Be very careful, then, how you live—not as unwise but as wise, making the most of every opportunity" (Eph. 5:15-16). The wise person makes the most of every opportunity he or she has. The Christian leader, then, must be time-conscious. That is, he must realize that time is his most valuable resource.

The leader concerned about making the most of his time should identify his personal time robbers and systematically work at eliminating them. A time robber is any controllable activity that hinders or delays your efforts to accomplish the job or task.

During a recent management seminar in Chicago, I asked thirty Christian leaders and executives to identify their time robbers. They most frequently mentioned:

- Procrastination

- Poor personal planning and scheduling

- Interruptions by people without appointments

- Poor delegation

- Poor use of the telephone

- Reading junk mail

- Lack of concern for good time management

- Lack of clear priorities

Time Inventory Sheet For Use In Identifying Time Robbers

What I plan to do tomorrow		What I actually did
_____	8:00	_____
_____	8:30	_____
_____	9:00	_____
_____	9:30	_____
_____	10:00	_____
_____	10:30	_____
_____	11:00	_____
_____	11:30	_____
_____	12:00	_____
_____	12:30	_____
_____	1:00	_____
_____	1:30	_____
_____	2:00	_____
_____	2:30	_____
_____	3:00	_____
_____	3:30	_____
_____	4:00	_____
_____	4:30	_____
_____	5:00	_____

How much time was used as scheduled?_____ Unscheduled?_____
What were the time robbers that got me off schedule? _____
_____
_____

Figure 12. A sample time inventory sheet designed to help identify personal time robbers.

How to Identify Your Personal Time Robbers

There is little value in being concerned about one's time robbers without having a method of identifying them. Figure 12 makes it possible for each person to clearly identify his time robbers.

The left side of the figure lists what is to be done on the following day at a specified time. At the bottom the individual records how much time was used as scheduled and how much time was used in some other way. Usually those activities that cause an individual to get off schedule can be considered time robbers.

How to Use a Time Inventory Sheet

Time management is unglamorous, hard work. As a result, most people who complain about how they manage their time are unwilling to pay the price to improve. The time inventory sheet is a simple but effective tool for beginning to improve one's management of time.

Allow three to five days to conduct the time inventory. The leader or manager should plan to use the time inventory sheet for three to five consecutive days in order to identify his most common time robbers.

Record the following day's activities. The first step in using the time inventory sheet is to record the following day's activities on the left side of the sheet under "What I plan to do tomorrow." Be specific in recording each activity. Vague statements make it more difficult to determine if you actually did what you planned to do. For example, if you have a meeting at 9 A.M. with the vice president of finance, don't just enter "meeting" at the 9:00 time slot. State exactly who the meeting is with and what is to be discussed.

The following day, record the activities as they are performed. This information is recorded on the right side of the page under "What I actually did today." Here again, be specific. Time robbers frequently hide disguised among legitimate activities. Therefore, it is extremely important to record everything you do during that time frame. This

149

will allow you to later study the various activities to determine if any of them should be considered time robbers.

Add the time worked as scheduled. At the end of the day, study the time inventory sheet to determine how much time was spent on scheduled activities and how much time was spent on unscheduled (but controllable) activities. Record the amount of scheduled and unscheduled time at the bottom of the sheet.

Deal with controllable and uncontrollable time. The controllable activities that cause a person to get off schedule should be considered time robbers and eliminated. However, uncontrollable activities, such as emergency meetings called by the boss, should be considered as part of the job. Even though they cause you to get off schedule, they should not be considered as time robbers.

How to Eliminate Time Robbers

Trying to eliminate time robbers can be a frustrating experience. Wasting time doesn't just happen; it is allowed to occur. In most cases it is the result of poor time-use habits. Therefore, eliminating time robbers frequently involves eliminating poor time-use habits. The single most difficult aspect of managing time more effectively is changing habits.

A habit usually develops over an extended period of time and generally becomes an unconscious action. As a result, habits that can be classified as time robbers usually are difficult to break. However, with patience and a strong commitment to make the most of his time, the leader or manager can become proficient in time management.

Develop and maintain an organized personal activity schedule. This is one of the most obvious—yet frequently neglected—tools of time management. A manager recently told me, "I hate making a schedule because it reveals how poorly I follow it."

An organized personal activity schedule tells a manager what he should be doing. However, it does not guarantee the activities will be done. A friend of mine is vice president of a Christian organization on the East Coast. The last time we were together, he said, "I keep making an activity schedule like you told me, but I can't find anyone to do all those things for me." Even though he was joking, he described the attitude many leaders have toward personal activity schedules.

Procedures for Developing a Weekly Activity Schedule

1. Make a list of next week's activities. This should include all of the manager's known activities.

2. Determine if each activity is to be done next week or during some future week. This does not mean the leader is procrastinating; it simply means he wants to make sure he identifies those to be done next week only.

3. Select only those activities to be done next week and determine which ones should be delegate.

4. Sort out all activities not assignable. This list represents the activities to be done by the manager or leader.

5. Set priorities for the activities.

6. Determine the amount of time to be allotted for the completion of each activity.

7. Delegate the activities to be performed by subordinates, giving them deadlines.

8. Assign a specific day on next week's calendar for each of your personal activities. You should also impose deadlines on yourself, even if none are required.

9. Conduct a follow-up at the end of the week to determine whether all projects were accomplished on schedule. If not, identify the time robbers that got you off schedule.

10. Prepare the following week's schedule by repeating steps 1 through 9.

Once the manager has developed a weekly schedule, he can begin breaking the week down into a daily schedule. For best results, the manager should keep his daily schedule in some type of portable pocket calendar. Several good ones are on the market and most office supply stores carry a wide selection.

Learn to schedule emergencies and interruptions in advance. Managers frequently become discouraged trying to maintain a schedule because of the numerous unavoidable emergencies and interruptions that occur. However, the best way to handle interruptions is to schedule them "before" they occur.

A friend of mine, Ed Thompson, is the president of a large service organization. One day I dropped by his office unannounced to see if he had time for a "quick cup of coffee." (I was about to become a time robber, right?) I was pleasantly surprised to find that he could fit me into his schedule.

As we chatted I asked him how he was able to fit me in his busy schedule without an appointment. "It's simple," he said with a smile. "I've learned to schedule interruptions like you in advance." When I asked him to explain what he meant by that, he continued, "Well, since unexpected emergencies and interruptions are part of a manager's life, I've learned to leave a block of time each morning and afternoon unscheduled in order to provide enough flexibility in my daily schedule to handle them. Then, if no interruption shows up, I have additional time to devote to my activities."

I learned a great deal about time management that day from my wise friend. Since then, I have been using his principle of scheduling interruptions in advance and have discovered it really works.

Figure 13 gives an example of unscheduled time available to handle emergencies and interruptions. Leave a block of time each morning and afternoon free to handle important things that come up unexpectedly. The amount of unscheduled time will vary depending on the type of activities in which the leader or manager is engaged. In this way, if you had planned to answer correspondence from 9 to 10 but the boss calls an unexpected meeting during that time, you can

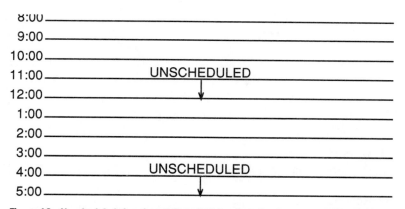

Figure 13. Unscheduled time in a daily schedule gives the manager an opportunity to deal with unexpected emergencies and still remain on schedule at the end of the day.

still be back on schedule by noon by using the unscheduled time between 11 and 12 to answer correspondence.

How to Set Priorities

Learning to set priorities is one of the most important, but sometimes difficult, aspects of effectively managing one's time. During the past several years our consulting firm has taught thousands of managers how to set priorities using the "Priority Scale," one of the most valuable priority setting tools available (see fig. 14).

Step One: In the upper left-hand corner of the priority scale under "List to Be Prioritized," record the items you wish to put in priority order.

Step Two: Compare item 1 (work on budget) with item 2 (prepare equipment report) and circle the one most important. Next, compare item 1 with item 3, then with item 4, and so on, circling the most important items.

Continue the process by moving one row to the right and comparing item 2 (preparing equipment report) with item 3 (scheduling trip and meeting with Bill). Then compare 2 with 4 and 2 with 5, each time circling the number most important. Next, compare 3 with 4 and 3 with 5. Finally, compare 4 with 5.

PRIORITY SCALE

List to be prioritized		Total circled
1. Work on budget		___1s
2. Prepare equipment report	1 2	___2s
3. Schedule trip & meeting with Bill	1 2 3 3	___3s
4. Work with secretary on new filing system	1 2 3 4 4 4	___4s
5. Conduct Mary's performance review	1 2 3 4 5 5 5 5	___5s
6.	1 2 3 4 5 6 6 6 6 6	___6s
7.	1 2 3 4 5 6 7 7 7 7 7	___7s
8.	1 2 3 4 5 6 7 8 8 8 8 8	___8s
9.	1 2 3 4 5 6 7 8 9 9 9 9 9 9 9 9	___9s
10.	1 2 3 4 5 6 7 8 9 10 10 10 10 10 10 10 10 10	___10s

Figure 14. The priority scale is one of the most effective priority-setting tools available.

Step Three: Once you have completed the comparison, add up the total number of 1s, 2s, 3s, 4s, and 5s and record them under "total circled," as illustrated.

Step Four: Now you are ready to rearrange—in order of priority—the items to be included in next week's work schedule. Since there were more 3s circled than any other number, you have established this as the highest priority. Therefore, write, "schedule meeting and trip with Bill" as your number one priority, as shown in figure 15. Since number 5 was second highest with three circled, it is recorded second.

Order of priority based on number circled
1. schedule trip & meeting with Bill
2. conduct Mary's performance review
3. work on budget
4. work with secretary on new filing system
5. prepare equipment report
6.
7.
8.
9.
10.

Figure 15. A list of priorities based on the priority scale.

The priority scale has many uses. However, there is little value in working a list of items through the priority scale if you ignore the results. An organization asked for our assistance in setting long-range planning priorities. We spent a day with the board of directors teaching them how to use the priority scale in the planning process. By the end of the day they had developed eight major priorities. Product development was their number one concern, and facility expansion was number eight. Six months later we returned to the organization on a consulting project and discovered they were pouring the foundation for a new facility, but they had not yet started on their top priority, product expansion.

This firm did not benefit from identifying priorities because emotions interfered with reality. The priority scale is designed to minimize the emotional impact when setting priorities. However, it is a waste of time to use the priority scale and let your emotions dictate your actions.

Avoid the Activity Trap

There is a great deal of difference between activity and accomplishment. An old gentleman once told his neighbor, "I sure worked hard today."

"Did you get a lot done?" his neighbor asked.

"No—just worked hard," the old gentleman replied.

I'm afraid many of us work hard, but at the end of the day or week discover we accomplished little. Many leaders and managers are like the old gentleman—they work hard, but seem to get little done. Part of the problem can be traced to the activity trap, which gets people involved in numerous tasks that do not contribute to the predetermined goal or objective.

The Bible tells of a servant given the job of watching a prisoner during a battle. The prisoner escaped, and when the servant was to explain what happened, he said, "While your servant was busy here and there, the man disappeared" (1 Kings 20:40). Notice the servant was busy. He was involved in lots of activity, but he failed to accomplish his goal, which was to guard the prisoner. In fact, it was the servant's numerous activities that caused him to fail.

Like that servant, many Christian leaders work from morning till night, but they never seem to get the important things done. The president of a missions organization recently told me, "If we could reach the world by holding meetings, every person would have become a Christian years ago." He went on to say, "We are so busy working, we can't do our job."

Important principles of time management appear in the account in Luke 10:38-42. Martha was a hard worker, constantly busy serving Jesus and the other guests in her home. However, her sister Mary, recognizing an opportunity to learn from Jesus' teachings, let the housework go and joined those listening to Jesus. Martha, angered at her sister's failure to help with the work, went to Jesus and complained, "Lord, don't You care that my sister has left me to do the work by myself?" (v. 40)

Martha was caught in an activity trap. She was "distracted by all the preparations that had to be made" (v. 40). Jesus recognized that and said, "Martha, Martha . . . you are worried and upset about many things, but only one thing is needed" (vv. 41-42).

What principles of time management are apparent in this passage? First, Martha was so busy she overlooked the important thing—the opportunity to learn from Jesus. Like Martha, people caught in an activity trap lose sight of the few important things and get caught up in the fury of action, motion, and work, assuming they are accomplishing something worthwhile.

Second, Martha was unaware she had lost sight of the goal, having become "distracted by all the preparations." This is a common pattern of those caught in an activity trap. Once we lose sight of the goal, we focus our efforts on activity—and that usually becomes our goal.

Third, Martha criticized her sister Mary because she wasn't as busy as Martha. People caught in an activity trap usually become deceived into thinking they are producing more than others because they are busier. As a result, they frequently complain about other people's lack of activity.

Fourth, Jesus pointed out that Martha's furious pace was creating stress within her. This tends to be the end result of the activity trap. The "busy" activities produce stress and tension, which frequently stimulate more and more activity.

Time management consultants say that 80 percent of the results are produced by 20 percent of the effort. This means that the other 80 percent of our effort only contributes 20 percent to the results. To avoid the activity trap, we must eliminate those activities that make little if any contribution to the goal. Adopting the following rules will help:

1. Avoid working on several small projects at once.

2. Finish one project before starting another.

3. Prioritize your projects and work on the most important ones first.

4. Set self-imposed deadlines for all projects and meet them.

5. Concentrate on results.

How to Stay on a Schedule

Organizing and scheduling time is hard work and time consuming; therefore, it is important to maintain the schedule once it is developed. To stay on schedule, first develop your priorities and make sure they are communicated. Second, learn to say no to things that do not contribute to the priority. And third, maintain a high level of commitment to managing your time effectively.

Develop priorities and make sure they are communicated. Undefined priorities are the worst time robbers and schedule breakers. Without priorities, people fall into the activity trap—spending their time on activities that do not contribute to their overall goals.

A manager told me, "We have priorities alright. The only problem is they are like the weather—they change every fifteen minutes." He went on to say, "The other day my boss called and informed me of an 'urgent project' that had to be done before the end of the day. Half an hour later he told me to stop working on that urgent project and start another." He continued, "A few calls like that and it doesn't take long to realize we really don't have any clear priorities."

I have heard similar stories from other frustrated employees who really don't know what their company's priorities are. As a result, they jump from one activity to another, frequently reacting to events that have little if any influence on their priorities.

Learn to say no to things that do not contribute to the priority. In order to maintain a schedule and eventually achieve priorities, the Christian leader must learn to say no to many worthwhile causes and requests. Generally speaking, the greater the priority, the more frequently one has to say no.

Jesus had constant demands on His time. Needy people were everywhere. However, in order to do what the Father directed, He had to decline some activities. A classic example of this is found in Mark 1:32-38. Jesus worked late into the night healing the sick and casting out demons. The next morning He got up before daylight and went out alone to pray. The disciples came to find Him and said, "Everyone is looking for You!" Jesus replied, "Let us go somewhere else—to the nearby villages—so I can preach there also. That is why I have come" (Mark 1:37-38).

Jesus never lost sight of His priorities. When demands on His time threatened to interfere with His Father's will, He quickly said no to those demands. Undoubtedly, there were still unmet needs back in the city. However, Jesus realized if He yielded to every request for His time, He would not have been able to visit the other communities in which He needed to minister.

There are many good activities that need to be done by someone. However, the Christian leader must realize he can't meet *all* of the needs of *all* of the people *all* of the time. He must set priorities and learn to say no in order to do the important things God has planned for him.

Maintain a high level of commitment to managing your time effectively. Effective time management is hard work. It usually involves breaking poor habits and replacing them with good ones.

Most leaders and managers draw up some sort of daily and weekly schedules, but only those committed to their schedules follow them. The manager must keep in mind the commitment isn't to the schedule, but to accomplishing the important goals and priorities he or she has set. The schedule is only the means to an end.

The Importance of Stressing Time Management

No one recognizes the value of using time wisely more than Jesus Christ. He knew He only had three years to train His disciples to carry on the great work of taking the Gospel to the whole world. Once, He told them, "As long as it is day, we must do the work of Him who sent Me. Night is coming, when no one can work" (John 9:4).

Jesus never lost sight of His goal. He worked diligently to insure He made the best possible use of His time. As a result He was able to say to the Father, "I have brought You glory on earth by completing the work You gave Me to do" (John 17:4).

Unfortunately, many modern Christian leaders fail to place the same importance on time that Jesus did. In fact, apathy regarding waste of time is one of the most serious sicknesses infecting our nation's organizations. A study conducted by Robert Half, a personnel consultant, revealed that in 1980 the average employee in America "stole" four hours and five minutes from his employer every week at an annual cost of $98 billion. (*U.S. News and World Report*, Feb. 23,1981).

Mr. Half indicated that top leadership is as guilty as the rank and file employee and concluded: "The problem, we believe, is so serious that every executive needs to give extra thought to ways of combating it in his or her own organization."

The Christian leader must take the initiative in stressing the importance of time management. He must set the example for his workers and encourage everyone to adopt Jesus' attitude: "As long as it is day, we must do the work of Him who sent Me. Night is coming, when no one can work"(John 9:4).

The Important Role of Timing

For the Christian leader, manager, and businessperson, God's timing plays a major role in time management. God not only has a plan for the Christian leader, He also has a timetable in which the plan is to be accomplished. "God will bring to judgment both the righteous and the wicked, for there will be a time for every activity, a time for every deed" (Ecc. 3:17).

Throughout His ministry, Jesus was aware of the importance of doing things in God's timing. He made decisions and took action according to God's timing (Luke 9:51; John 2:4).

At the end of His ministry, He told His disciples, "Go into the city to a certain man and tell him, 'The Teacher says: My appointed time is near. I am going to celebrate the Passover with my disciples at your house'" (Matt. 26:18). In the Garden of Gethsemane, Jesus told His disciples, "Look, the hour is near, and the Son of Man is betrayed into the hands of sinners" (Matt. 26:45).

A leader committed to letting God work His will through him will be sensitive to God's timing. The effective use of time consists of doing what God wants at the time He wants it done.

Chapter Summary

The Bible challenges the Christian leader to make the most of his time. Time is our most important resource. It can't be saved or stored—only used. Time is the passing of life. Therefore, the person having problems managing time is actually having difficulty managing his or her life.

In order to manage your time more effectively, begin identifying your time robbers. A time robber is any controllable activity that hinders or delays your efforts to accomplish a job or task. Most time robbers can easily be identified by using a time inventory sheet for three to five consecutive days.

161

Every leader should maintain a daily and weekly schedule. This is one of the best ways to avoid time robbers and activity traps. When setting schedules make sure the top priorities are first. The priority scale is an excellent priority setting tool and should be used regularly in determining one's priorities. Priorities help keep the leader or manager on schedule, making it easier to say no to requests that can lead to activity traps.

For the Christian leader, God's timing plays a major role in time management. The Bible points out that God has His own schedule. Jesus recognized this and worked to make sure His decisions and actions correspond with God's timetable. Therefore, the Christian leader must seek God's guidance concerning when a project should be implemented and then use the available time wisely.

Personal Application

Use the time inventory sheet to determine your personal time robbers.

Follow the steps outlined in this chapter to develop a weekly and daily schedule. Use the priority scale regularly for determining personal priorities.

Teach those in your department or organization how to use the priority scale and begin encouraging others to focus on effective time management.

When planning schedules, seek God's timing for the activity or project.

CHAPTER 11

ATTITUDE AND PERFORMANCE

At the conclusion of a management seminar, a young man told me, "I don't think these principles will work in my department."

"You're right," I said. "They probably won't."

He gave me a puzzled look and said, "But you just told us they would work in any organization. Now you're contradicting yourself."

It was obvious he was becoming quite irritated with me, so I said, "No, I'm not contradicting myself. They probably won't work for you because you don't think they will work. Therefore, you probably won't make the commitment needed for them to work."

Our Attitudes Greatly Influence Our Actions

The Bible says, "As water reflects a face, so a man's heart reflects the man" (Prov. 27:19). And in Proverbs 23:7 we are told that as a person "thinketh in his heart, so is he" (KJV). These verses suggest the powerful influence our thoughts have over our actions.

The Christian leader's attitude plays a major role in determining what he or she does and achieves. If a person thinks something is impossible, he usually doesn't bother to try doing it. Thus the thoughts frequently become a self-fulfilling prophecy.

One of the best case studies concerning the influence people's thoughts have on their actions is recorded in Numbers 13. Moses sent out twelve spies to determine the lay of the land, the size and strength of the cities, and the type of crops raised (vv. 17-20). Moses did not ask the spies to determine whether it was possible to invade the land. Their mission was to discover what conditions would prevail when the invasion occurred.

The spies spent forty days in the land and came back with a glowing report concerning its fertility and abundant produce. They began by saying, "We went into the land to which you sent us, and it does flow with milk and honey!" (Num. 13:27)

However, most of the spies quickly turned their attention to the military might of the inhabitants. "But the people who live there are powerful, and the cities are fortified and very large. We even saw descendants of Anak there"(v. 28). The longer they dwelled on the negative, the more negative they became. Finally, ten of the twelve spies said, "We can't attack those people; they are stronger than we are" (v. 31).

They concluded, "The land we explored devours those living in it" (v. 32). The longer the spies talked and listened to their own negative thoughts, the more convinced they became that it was impossible to invade the land. They said, "We seemed like grasshoppers in our own eyes, and we looked the same to them" (v. 33).

Negative thinking always produces negative assumptions and conclusions. Because they thought they were like grasshoppers beside the enemy, the spies imagined the enemy also thought they were like grasshoppers. However, the Book of Joshua reveals this was a false assumption produced entirely by the spies' own negative thought pattern.

The spies' negative report spread like wildfire among the people of Israel and they cried all night saying, "If only we had died in Egypt! Or in this desert! Why is the Lord bringing us to this land only to let us fall by the sword?" (Num. 14:2-3)

Negative attitudes are highly contagious. It wasn't long before the negative thinking of the ten spies infected the entire nation.

As a result, their negative thoughts produced negative actions. For the next thirty-eight years that entire generation of negative thinkers wandered around in the wilderness until they all died. They never took the land God promised them because they didn't think they could.

Some thirty-eight years later, that generation of negative thinkers had been replaced by their children, under the leadership of Joshua. Once again the people of Israel came to the banks of the Jordan River and looked across to the other side, to the Promised Land that God had wanted to give to their parents years earlier. Again spies were sent out. They went to Jericho and spent the night at a house owned by a prostitute named Rahab.

Rahab recognized the spies as Israelites by the clothes they wore. She told them the people in the city were terrified of them because of the way God fought for them. She said, "We have heard how the Lord dried up the water of the Red Sea for you . . . and what you did to . . . the two kings of the Amorites . . . When we heard of it, our hearts sank and everyone's courage failed because of you" (Josh. 2:10-11).

Keep in mind that these people in Jericho who are so afraid of Israel are the children of those who a generation before had first heard of Israel and their great God. Think of how terrified their parents must have been then. And imagine, Israel's negative thinking caused them to feel like grasshoppers and to retreat from the Promised Land to spend the rest of their lives wandering in the wilderness until that entire generation of negative thinker died.

This new detachment of spies took their report from Rahab back to Joshua and the people of Israel and said, "The Lord has surely given the whole world into our hands; all the people are melting in fear because of us" (Josh. 2:24).

This time the spies maintained a positive outlook and gave a positive report. This motivated the people to take positive action, and within a few days they had taken the city of Jericho.

What was the difference between this generation of Israelites and their parents? God hadn't changed. He had actually given the land to the people thirty-eight years before. However, the negative thinking had caused them to take flight instead of taking the land. The difference was attitude.

Tale of Two Attitudes

The Christian leader or businessperson must keep in mind that the power of negative thinking is just as great as the power of positive thinking. Negative thinking is one of Satan's most effective tools. If he can cause you to form negative thoughts and attitudes, he knows he will get negative results from your actions, thus weakening your—and your organization's—productivity.

Two friends of mine, we'll call them Dave and Harry, are presidents of Christian organizations. Dave is the head of a large, progressive, missions-oriented organization with a vision to reach the entire world with the message of Jesus Christ, using every possible means of modern communication. He recently told me, "My job is to learn to think as big as God thinks—and God thinks in terms of every person in every country."

As we talked, Dave went on to say, "We are living in exciting times. God is enabling us to expand our ministry greatly through modern technology." He began describing plans to get the Gospel into every major city in the world by way of satellite communication. He explained how they intended to enlarge their facilities and add new staff for the ministry.

During my time with Dave's organization, I talked with many of his staff, all of whom were equally excited about the general things God was doing through their organization.

As I commented to one of the organization's managers about how excited and motivated the people were, he said, "Dave has helped us begin to realize we have a big God who wants to get the Gospel literally to every person. Therefore, we aren't afraid to trust God for big things."

A few days later I was with my friend Harry, also the president of a missions-oriented organization. During one of our discussions he said, "You know, Myron, we are living in very trying and difficult times. It is getting harder and harder to get the Gospel into some countries, and inflation is making it very difficult to send and keep missionaries on the field." He explained how his organization was making a major effort to cut back on some of their objectives and projects in an effort to save money.

As we talked, I couldn't help but notice the difference in his and Dave's attitudes. I asked some of Harry's staff how they felt about the future of the organization's ministry. One staff person summed up the feelings of the others when he said, "We are going to have to learn to tighten our belts and cut back on several of our long-range plans, because we just can't afford to send and support as many missionaries as we once could."

As I left Harry's group, I was reminded of the difference between the attitude of the ten spies sent out by Moses and the attitude of those sent out by Joshua. I realized a similar comparison could be made between Dave's and Harry's organizations. One had a positive attitude, believing God would meet their every need. The other looked at circumstances instead of God and concluded most of their goals could not be achieved.

An executive in a Christian organization recently said, "I don't understand why _____ (Christian organization) is able to get one of their donors to give a $7 million gift to them and we struggle to get a $7,000 gift."

I smiled at him and said, "Maybe it's because you haven't learned to believe God for a $7 million project."

He hung his head and replied, "You know, you're right. Our entire budget isn't $7 million."

The human mind is the most important battlefield because our thoughts and attitudes greatly influence our actions. Therefore, Satan works overtime trying to convince us to think negatively, to doubt God, and to rely on our feelings instead of the facts in God's Word.

God also wants control of our minds. Thus Paul exhorts us "to be made new in the attitude of your minds; and to put on the new self, created to be like God in true righteousness and holiness" (Eph. 4:23-24).

The Size of Your Goal Reflects the Size of Your God

The "power of positive thinking" promotes the concept that by thinking positively, an individual can turn desires into reality. Even though our attitudes greatly influence our actions, we must not be deceived into believing that our own mental power is sufficient to accomplish all our plans—which is the philosophy of many of those who religiously promote the power of positive thinking.

God makes it clear that man—left to himself—has very little power over many of his circumstances. "This is what the Lord says: 'Cursed is the one who trusts in man, who depends on flesh for his strength and whose heart turns away from the Lord. He will be like a bush in the wastelands; he will not see prosperity when it comes. He will dwell in the parched places of the desert, and a salt land where no one lives'" (Jer. 17:5-6).

This passage clearly illustrates the fallacy of trusting solely in human resources and resourcefulness to solve problems and achieve one's goals. However, the same passage continues, "But blessed is the man who trusts in the Lord, whose confidence is in Him. He will be like a tree planted by the water that sends out its roots by the stream. It does not fear when heat comes; its leaves are always green. It has no worries in a year of drought and never fails to bear fruit" (vv. 7-8).

What a vivid contrast between the person who trusts self and the one trusting God. The power of positive thinking focuses on human resourcefulness while the power of godly thinking focuses on God as the total resource.

Therefore, the Christian leader's positive attitudes should stem from godly thinking, from recognizing that God is the total resource for achieving the plan or project. How much of God's power is available to the Christian leader? "Now glory be to God Who by His mighty power at work within us is able to do far more than we would ever dare to ask or even dream of—infinitely beyond our highest prayers, desires, thoughts, or hopes" (Eph. 3:20, TLB).

What a description of the amount of God's power available to us! We can't think thoughts great enough or pray prayers big enough to tap all of God's power. That should be the source of the Christian leader's positive thinking.

Show me a person with small goals and I will show you a person with a small God. The size of our goals reflects the size of our God. For example, a friend of mine started a Christian camp in the Rocky Mountains of Colorado. It was a beautiful setting—high, snow-capped peaks, beautiful mountain meadows, and a clear, cold trout stream running beside tall, green pine trees.

One day I visited my friend's camp and got the shock of my life. As he gave me the personalized tour, we stopped in front of a row of rusty, worn-out trailer houses. My friend said, "Now, Myron, there is an answer to prayer." He explained that he had asked God for some used trailers for dormitories and several people had donated these for the use of camp guests.

As we continued our tour, my friend showed me a dilapidated, World War II Quonset hut being used as a chapel and dining hall. Again we stopped to admire another answer to prayer.

"You know," he said, "I told God that surely someone had a building they could donate to the camp, and here it is. Just what we need for a meeting place."

At the end of the tour I was shown several outdated vehicles and an old dump truck.

"I told God there was an extra truck out there somewhere that wasn't being used, and sure enough, a contractor donated that truck to us."

As I looked over these facilities, the thought kept going through my mind, "Is God really this poor?" This certainly didn't fit the description of the God "able to do far more than we would even dare ask." However, my friend said, "Isn't God great? All the things were on my prayer list, and God provided them all."

Then I remembered Mark 11:24. "Therefore I tell you, whatever you ask for in prayer, believe that you have received it, and it will be yours." God can produce more than we are capable of thinking of or asking for. However, we must do the asking, and what we say is what we get.

Our concept of God determines what we ask for and believe God will provide. The camp owner believed God would provide second-hand junk, so that is what he prayed for and received. However, Dave, the president of the missions organization, is seeing God bring in millions of dollars for the Gospel, provide for new facilities, and enlarge his staff. What is the difference? Part of the difference is in their concept of God and what He will do. Their concepts of God and attitudes toward Him influenced what they were willing to pray for and trust God to provide. In other words, the size of their God was reflected in the size of their goals.

If you want to know how big your God is, look at the size of your goals and what you are asking God to do. We never ask God for more than we think He is capable of providing.

Paul wasn't a great missionary because he was a great man; he was a great missionary because he had a great God. He shared the secret to successful living when he informed the people in Ephesus that God was putting His great power in His people to accomplish things greater then they could ask or think. Realizing the greatness of God helps us to expand our own thoughts and plans concerning what He wants to accomplish through us.

The Bible Commands Us to Think Positively

We read in Philippians 4:8, "Finally, brothers, whatever is true, whatever is noble, whatever is right, whatever is pure, whatever is lovely, whatever is admirable—if anything is excellent or praiseworthy—think about such things." This verse emphasizes that we should be filling our minds with positive thoughts.

The mind is like a computer. It stores and retrieves information. As figure 16 illustrates, our mind is divided into two parts, the conscious and the subconscious. Events "a" and "b" enter the conscious section of the mind where value judgment determines whether they are positive or negative. The event is then stored in the subconscious section of the mind as a positive or negative event which can be sent

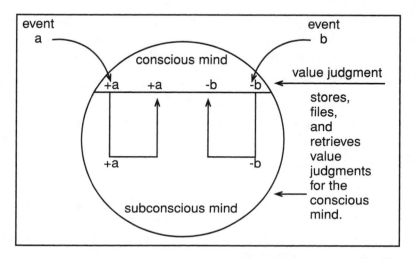

Figure 16. The mind has two parts—conscious and unconscious. The conscious makes value judgments concerning what is negative or positive and stores the information in the subconscous mind where it can be retrieved if needed.

back to the conscious section when needed. As a result, attitudes formed from past events greatly influence one's actions in the future.

For example, if an employee's conscious mind develops a negative attitude, thinking that the boss really isn't interested in his ideas, that attitude is stored in the subconscious. If the boss later asks for ideas, the employee's subconscious sends the conscious mind the message, "The boss really isn't interested in my ideas." As a result, he probably will remain silent.

Negative thinking tends to discourage action and innovative ideas. That is why Scripture tells us to think on things that are true, noble, right, pure, lovely, admirable, and worthy of praise—these are all positive and tend to promote future innovative and positive actions.

The Keys to Maintaining a Positive Mental Attitude

Focus on God instead of self. In the account in Numbers 13, the majority of the spies focused on their personal resourcefulness instead of on God's resources. As a result, they developed negative thinking patterns. On the other hand, in the account in Joshua 2, the spies said, "The Lord has surely given the whole land into our hands" (v. 24). This attitude produced positive action.

Much later, in the days of King Saul, the Israelite army was confronted by Goliath, a giant over nine feet tall. "When the Israelites saw the man, they all ran from him in great fear" (1 Sam. 17:24). They compared their individual strength with Goliath's, and as a result, developed fearful and negative thought patterns.

However, David, the young shepherd, said, "Who is this uncircumcised Philistine that he should defy the armies of the living God?" (v. 26) David compared Goliath to God and concluded the giant was no match for the Creator of the universe.

David's reliance on God allowed him to maintain a positive and confident attitude when facing Goliath. He said, "You come against me with sword and spear and javelin, but I come against you in the name of the Lord Almighty, the God of the armies of Israel, whom you have defied. This day the Lord will hand you over to me, and I'll strike you down and cut off your head" (vv. 45-46). David's focus on God allowed him to keep a positive mental attitude even when facing a man over nine feet tall who was trying to kill him.

Many leaders, managers, and businesspeople allow their attitudes to be controlled by circumstances. A businessman's wife once told me, "My husband's attitude is controlled by the stock market—when stocks go up he's in a good mood, but when they go down, he's a grouch."

By contrast Paul wrote, "I know what it is to be in need, and I know what it is to have plenty. I have learned the secret of being content in any and every situation, whether well fed or hungry, whether living in plenty or in want. I can do everything through Him who gives me strength" (Phil. 4:12-13). Paul learned that the key to a positive attitude was to focus on God in every situation—not on self and circumstances. The stock market may go up or down, but God never changes. His promises are consistently true, providing security in every situation.

Look to the future, not the past. A study of Paul's life reveals numerous principles concerning how to maintain a positive, optimistic attitude and outlook on life. One of these principles is to look to the future with anticipation. "One thing I do: Forgetting what is behind and straining toward what is ahead, I press on toward the goal to win the prize for which God has called me heavenward in Christ Jesus" (Phil. 3:13-14). Once Paul began focusing on God and His resources instead of personal resourcefulness, the future became exciting and challenging. Paul eagerly looked to the future, anticipating what God was going to do in and through him.

Paul also refused to dwell on the past, whether on his failures or his achievements. Instead, he focused on the present and maintained an eager anticipation of the future. The Christian leader should use Paul's life as a model, eagerly anticipating what God plans to do with and through him.

Always have a goal. Paul did. He said, "I press on toward the goal" (Phil. 3:14). A goal keeps us oriented toward achievement and success—important ingredients in maintaining positive attitudes. Goals give meaning to life and reason for working. People with goals rarely ask, "Who am I and why am I here?"

View problems as an opportunity for improvement. We are all vulnerable to negative attitudes and thinking when faced with a problem. However, James writes, "Dear brothers, is your life full of difficulties and temptations? Then be happy" (James 1:2, TLB).

That seems like a ridiculous statement. Why should we be happy when facing difficulty? The answer is given in the next verse: "For when the way is rough, your patience has a chance to grow" (v. 3). Here we have an important principle for maintaining a positive attitude: *A problem always brings an opportunity for improvement.*

The leader's attitudes play a major role in the outcome of a project. While trying to develop the incandescent lamp, Thomas Edison and his lab partners experienced great difficulty and hundreds of failures. Each new problem became more frustrating to Edison's lab assistants, and they developed very negative attitudes toward the project.

Finally, Edison's lab partners approached him and said, "Tom, why don't we give up on the idea? We've tried hundreds of experiments and none of them has worked. Let's face it; the thing is a failure."

Edison replied, "We haven't failed once. We now know hundreds of things that won't work, so we're just that much closer to the right answer."

Edison was a great inventor because he learned to view problems as opportunities for advancement. Therefore, he was able to maintain a positive attitude, which helped him develop workable solutions. On the other hand, his lab partners allowed the problems to generate negative attitudes, which caused them to want to abandon the project.

Since negative attitudes produce negative actions and positive attitudes produce positive actions, it is important for the leader or manager to remain positive when dealing with problems. This is best achieved by recognizing that every problem brings with it the opportunity for improvement.

Attitudes Are Contagious

We have probably all heard the expression, "One bad apple can spoil the whole box." That cliché vividly describes the contagious nature of attitudes. One individual's negative attitude can infect an entire organization.

God was very much aware of the influence one person's negative attitudes could have on an entire group. Therefore, when He gave the Children of Israel their laws of military service, He said that prior to going into battle the officers should ask, "Is anyone afraid? If you are, go home before you frighten the rest of us!" (Deut. 20:8 TLB) This verse illustrates how contagious attitudes are.

The leader or manager must continually be aware of the morale and attitudes within his group or organization. He or she must be sensitive to individual feelings because they can quickly become the feelings of the entire department or organization.

Chapter Summary

Attitudes play a major role in determining your performance and the performance of your organization. As a man "thinketh in his heart, so is he" (Pro. 23:7, KJV). Positive attitudes contribute to positive results. On the other hand, negative attitudes contribute to negative actions and results.

The impact that attitudes have on actions is vividly illustrated in the accounts of Moses and Joshua sending out spies to check conditions in the Promised Land. Moses' spies came back believing it was impossible to take the land. As a result the land was not taken. However, Joshua's spies believed it was possible to take the land and the land was taken.

The Christian's approach to the power of positive thinking differs from the non-Christian's viewpoint. The Christian is able to have a positive attitude because he realizes God's power is the source of the accomplishment. On the other hand, the non-Christian believes the power of his own positive thoughts is enough to create the positive results.

The Christian leader's ability to think positively is greatly influenced by his concept of God. In fact, our goals are in direct proportion to the size of our God. We never trust God for more than we think He will do. One of the great tragedies is that God stands ready to do far more than we think, pray, or dream. This is evident when we read, "Now glory be to God who by His mighty power at work within us is able to do far more than we would ever dare to ask or even dream of—infinitely beyond our highest prayers, desires, thoughts, or hopes" (Eph. 3:20, TLB).

You don't develop positive attitudes simply by telling yourself to think positive thoughts. In order to maintain a positive outlook, always focus on God and His resources instead of your personal resourcefulness. Look to the future instead of the past. Always have clearly defined goals. And view your problems as opportunities for improvement.

Personal Application

Identify the positive and negative attitudes that currently exist within your department.

How are the negative attitudes affecting the productivity of your group or department?

What contributions have you made to the development of your group's positive attitudes? Negative attitudes?

How can the negative attitudes be eliminated?

What could be done to create a more positive work environment within your department?

CHAPTER 12

PERFORMANCE EVALUATION

I was discussing performance evaluation systems with the president of a Christian organization. "Of all the management activities I perform," he said, "I dislike conducting employee performance evaluations most." As we talked he explained that he always felt uncomfortable conducting the review and had some mistrust of the system they were using. "I'm not sure the form we use really tells us all that much about the actual performance of the employee," he said. "I sometimes wonder why we even use it."

Most performance evaluation systems do not accomplish what they should. As a result, people view them with some skepticism and disfavor. Dwight Shank, former production manager of one of the nation's leading rubber companies, told me, "In all the years I've worked in manufacturing management, every performance evaluation system I have used—or that has been used to evaluate me—has created controversy between managers and subordinates and has done more harm than good."

Betty Simpson, the personnel director for a hospital, recently told me, "Oh yes, we go through the motions of conducting employee performance evaluations, but everyone around here knows they don't really mean anything."

Most leaders and managers view performance evaluation systems in an unfavorable light. At best they are frequently seen as time-wasting activities that have little meaning or value. As a result, most managers resent having to fill out forms and conduct the sessions involved in complying with the system.

The Purpose of Performance Evaluation Systems

Regardless of what many leaders and managers think, employee performance evaluation systems were not designed simply to give the personnel department something to do. It is unfortunately true, however, that many of them have degenerated to little more than that. Nevertheless, to accomplish activities and projects as planned, the manager and employee must be able to evaluate progress and take corrective action as needed. This is the major purpose and function of the performance evaluation system.

Of all the tools at the manager's disposal, the performance evaluation is one of the most important and valuable. When properly designed and executed, it becomes the vehicle through which the organization's philosophy of management is communicated, trust is established, decision-making power is transferred, mistakes are turned into positive learning experiences, proper recognition is given, and both subordinate's and supervisor's productivity are increased.

When conducted properly, the performance evaluation system helps build strong teamwork and effective communication between managers and their employees. It serves the work-related needs of both the supervisor and subordinate. It helps develop and maintain two-way accountability between the manager and employee. Finally, it provides written records of the progress being made in accomplishing a project.

God's View of Performance

God is performance-conscious. Scripture indicates His concern about the quality and level of our work performance by saying, "Work hard and cheerfully at all you do, just as though you were working for the Lord and not merely for your masters" (Col. 3:23, TLB). While on earth, Jesus apparently performed to the best of His ability, for those observing His actions commented, "He has done everything well" (Mark 7:37).

When Jesus told the Parable of the Talents (Matt. 25), He described two types of people—those with good performance and those with bad. When describing the workers with good performance the master said, "Well done, good and faithful servant!" (v. 21) But when talking to the unproductive worker, the master said, "You wicked, lazy servant!" (v. 26)

The Christian leader should be committed to a high level and quality of performance. As we read in Colossians 3:23, we are to work hard and cheerfully at all we do. The Christian's goal is high performance with a positive and cheerful attitude toward the task being performed.

This is diametrically opposed to most of the world's view of work and performance. The secular philosophy tends to be "take it easy" and "don't work too hard." Many people are committed to doing only what is required to get by in order to keep the boss off their backs. This certainly is contrary to the standard established in Colossians 3:23.

Since God desires that we perform well, the Christian community and its leaders should strive for high performance. When properly developed and maintained, the performance evaluation system can be one of the best management tools for achieving and maintaining high performance.

Why Employee Performance Evaluation Systems Tend to Fail

Most employee performance evaluation systems are built on the wrong objectives. Most organizational performance evaluation systems are designed to evaluate past history instead of work currently in progress. They focus on the employee's past twelve months of work. Such performance systems are usually referred to as "annual reviews."

Once each year the supervisor fills out some type of performance review form that summarizes the employee's past year's performance. It is history, and it can't be changed. Except for the minimal value such a system offers for future planning purposes, the information has little purpose.

While discussing annual review systems at a seminar, a manager said, "I am reluctant to record that one of my employees had substandard performance for the past year because that really means I did a substandard job of supervising that person. Therefore, I tend to give all of my people favorable 'grades' because I figure if I make them look good, it makes me look good to my boss."

Another manager commented, "I learned the thing to do is always start an employee off with fairly low marks. That way I have lots of room to show improvement in his performance year after year." He concluded with, "I think it also makes the employee feel he is constantly improving."

As I listened to these remarks, I realized that filling out annual review forms was nothing more than a game to many managers. Most learn how to play the game so that everyone is happy, but it has little to do with the actual performance of the employee.

In order to be meaningful, a performance evaluation system should allow the manager and employee to take corrective action while the project is in progress. Since it is impossible to change past actions and performance, the annual review approach becomes meaningless in terms of helping people with a given project. Therefore, instead of focusing on evaluating past history or performance, the evaluation system should evaluate current projects in progress.

Most performance evaluation systems lack clearly defined performance standards. The typical employee performance evaluation system fails not only because it evaluates past history, but also because it lacks clearly defined standards by which performance is evaluated.

Ill-defined performance standards frequently generate frustration, confusion, and resentment in both supervisor and subordinate.

Dwight Shank explained it this way, "Performance standards on annual review forms are just too vague. I never know how to rate employees on things such as quality of work because we in management have never specifically identified what 'average quality' means."

He said, "What it usually boils down to is the manager's opinion versus the subordinate's, and that kind of situation usually leads to an unpleasant performance review."

While I was conducting an organizational analysis for a Christian organization, an employee asked me, "Why don't you tell our bosses to explain what they really mean by 'ability to work well with others'?" He said that he had recently received his annual review and his boss gave him a below average score on the category "ability to work well with others."

"I get along fine with everyone on the job," he continued. "But after that grade, I may not continue getting along very well with my boss. Tell me, how can we do what they want, if we don't know what they want us to do?"

The performance evaluation system should help both the supervisor and his employee agree on a definition of the performance standards *before* the employee starts working on a project in which his performance will be evaluated. If an employee is expected to do a "good" job, then he should know ahead of time what is meant by "good." Unless performance standards are clearly defined, with measurable terminology, employees have no way of knowing what is expected from them.

Most managers lack training in how to conduct meaningful performance review sessions with their employees. This is one of the major weaknesses with most employee performance review systems. It causes discomfort and anxiety for both the supervisor and his employees.

One day while I was working as a personnel director for an electronics manufacturing firm, a young lady came into my office with tears in her eyes. She said she felt like a schoolgirl who had just come from the principal's office.

When I asked what was the matter, she said she had just come from her first performance evaluation session with her new boss and felt like quitting. "If I was doing such a bad job, she should have said something sooner," she complained. "How was I to know she wasn't happy with my work?" As she chewed on her fingernails, she continued. "She treated me like I was her little girl who needed a spanking. I'm an adult, and the least she can do is treat me like one."

Similar scenes have been repeated countless times in personnel offices all across the country following performance evaluation reviews. Few managers know how to conduct a performance review session and give the type of constructive criticism that will be helpful to their employees.

As a result, many managers and organizations have stopped conducting performance evaluation interviews. One company I worked with decided to send out an annual form letter to all employees instead of conducting performance reviews. One of the firm's managers said, "The form letter saves the company thousands of dollars because we aren't wasting time in meaningless meetings."

I was curious as to how this annual letter system worked, so I asked several of the employees about it. One employee said, "Well, they send us this annual 'good guy' letter about appreciating our service to the company for another year—and that's about all it says." Some of the employees admitted they never read it because it really didn't mean anything. One employee said, "They just send it because they think they should say something about how the year went. Personally, I think they should save the stamp."

In order for performance evaluation interviews to be meaningful, they must be conducted in an environment that stimulates "two-way learning." That is, the supervisor needs to learn how he can better serve the work-related needs of the employee, and the employee needs to learn how he is doing at achieving the project as planned. The performance evaluation interview should never be a session that just evaluates the subordinate's performance. Each session should focus on the supervisor's performance as well.

Designing an Effective Performance Evaluation System

The following steps should be taken when setting up a performance evaluation system:

- Emphasize work in progress rather than evaluating past history through the use of annual reviews.

- The supervisor and subordinate should develop and agree on measurable performance standards. This should be done before the project or activity begins so that the subordinate will know by what standard his performance is being judged.

- The evaluation sessions should be done in a two-way learning environment. The supervisor's, as well as the subordinate's, performance should be considered. The emphasis should be on identifying and meeting all the needs that exist in order for the project to be accomplished as planned.

Evaluating Work in Progress

The Book of Nehemiah is replete with management and leadership principles. Nehemiah was the type of leader who created a work environment that motivated people to high levels of productivity.

In the fourth chapter of Nehemiah, we see him evaluating work in progress, not after the project was completed. As conditions changed, the work processes were also changed to meet existing needs. For example, at one point the people began to grow weak from the heavy work and their enemies threatened to attack the city. When this occurred, Nehemiah rearranged the people's work schedule and duties in order for them to get more rest and at the same time provide better defense for the city and workers (vv. 10-23). Had Nehemiah been satisfied to wait until the project was finished to evaluate the results, changing conditions might have prevented the people from completing the wall.

In order for an organization to accomplish its plan, it must follow whatever course of action is needed as conditions and circumstances change. Therefore, the organization must have some means of quickly identifying changing conditions and circumstances. The work-in-progress performance evaluation system is such a tool. It insures that the various activities within a project are being evaluated as the project is being done, not after it is over. In this way changing conditions and needs are quickly identified and corrective actions can be planned and implemented.

Developing a Work-in-Progress Evaluation Form

The fist step toward efficient performance evaluation is to prepare individual file folders for each employee. Next, take a blank sheet of paper and draw a line through the middle of the page from top or bottom, as shown in figure 17. Before meeting with the employee, write the person's name, position, department, and the date at the top of the page.

This first meeting gives the supervisor an opportunity to communicate to the employee that together they will determine the objectives and projects to be accomplished. It also involves the employee in participating in the development of the performance standards by which the employee will be evaluated.

Setting Performance Schedules

Many of the problems associated with performance evaluation systems can be traced to inadequate performance standards. Without clearly defined performance standards, the evaluation sessions become purely subjective. Performance standards allow the supervisor and employee to identify acceptable and unacceptable performance before the work begins.

PERFORMANCE AND EVALUATION

Employee name_____ Title_____

Department_____ Supervisor's name_____

Date prepared_____ Review date_____

The following information should be jointly prepared by the supervisor and the subordinate.

1. What are the specific objectives the employee will accomplish? State objectives in measurable terms.

2. By what performance standards will the employee be evaluated?

3. The next review date is:

_____

The following information will be recorded during the review session.

1. The current status of the progress being made on each project or objective.

2. Any changes in the work procedures needed to accomplish the project as previously planned, or changes in planned work required because of changing conditions.

3. Assistance needed by supervisor in order for the employee to accomplish his work.

4. Final evaluation of project once all work is completed.

Employee's signature

_____

Supervisor's signature

_____

Figure 17. A sample employee evaluation sheet.

Figure 18 illustrates the importance of establishing performance standards. The goal is to hit the bull's-eye as illustrated by arrow "A". However, suppose we miss the bull's-eye, but hit close to it in the first ring, as shown by arrow "B". Is that close enough, if we can hit there consistently? And what if we consistently hit in the second ring away from the bull's-eye, as shown by arrow "C"? Is that close enough? Or do we need to keep practicing until we can hit the bull's-eye with every shot? Is it realistic to set such a performance standard?

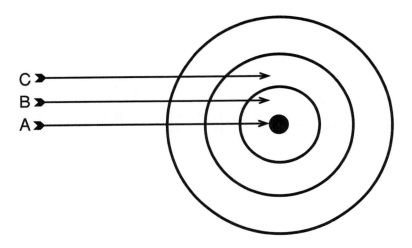

Figure 18. Performance standards should be clearly understood.

This is the type of question the performance standard answers. The goal with every shot is obviously to hit the bull's-eye. However, we must decide how far away from the bull's-eye is acceptable.

Therefore, when setting performance standards, the supervisor and employee should set both *preferred performance standards and minimum performance standards*. Preferred performance standards are what we are striving to achieve. However, if we would actually be willing to settle for less, the minimum performance standards tell us how far below the preferred standard we may go before repeating the activity or project becomes necessary. In other words, the minimum performance standards indicate how much tolerance exists within the standards.

As indicated earlier, the employee and the supervisor should work together to set the performance standards before the project begins. This will allow the employee to know exactly what is expected of him and will aid both the supervisor and the employee in evaluating work in progress. In addition, it will help the employee develop more pride in workmanship because he not only performed the task, but actually helped determine how well the project was to be done.

Implementing a Work-in-Progress Review System

Work-in-progress performance review is not something the manager does once a year and then forgets until the next year. On the contrary, the system is used in an ongoing manner as the employee works on the various tasks and projects associated with his job.

Figure 19 serves as an example of how a work-in-progress review might be done on a six-month project. The work-in-progress reviews are designed to keep the employee and supervisor informed concerning how the project is going, whether changes need to made, and whether the project is accomplishing the original objectives. The review sessions also insure open communication between the supervisor and employee concerning the various aspects of the project.

Conducting the Performance Evaluation Sessions

The evaluation session is an excellent vehicle for demonstrating to employees that management is committed to meeting their work-related needs. It also gives the supervisor a chance to establish a trust relationship with his subordinates. In addition, it becomes the setting for delegating decision-making power to employees and helping them turn failures and mistakes into positive learning experiences. It is a time, too, when the employee receives positive recognition for work accomplished and constructive criticism as needed.

Focus on developing a two-way learning environment. If the evaluation session is to be meaningful, the manager must avoid dealing only with the subordinate's performance. Instead, he must create an

0 • Meet with the emplyee to set measurable objectives and performance standards for the project.

1 week • The employee begins work on the project.

4 weeks • The supervisor and employee have the first work-in-progress review session. This session should be conducted shortly after the project begins in order to make sure there are no unexpected problems in implementing the start-up phase of the work. During this session, evaluate how realistic the objectives, time tables, and performance standards are. The supervisor should place a special emphasis on trying to identify the unforeseen work needs of the employee as he pursues the project. Set the date for the next review session. The length of time between review sessions will depend on how well the project is going.

12 weeks • The second work-in-progress review session should consider the remaining activities needed to complete the project on time. Is the project on schedule or not? Are new circumstances developing that weren't anticipated?

22 weeks • The third work-in-progress review of this project is conducted shortly before the end to make sure no last-minute changes are needed in order to complete the project as scheduled.

24 weeks • The final evaluation is conducted at the end of the project. This session compares the results with the original projections.

Figure 19. This graph illustrates a sample work-in-process performance evaluation review schedule on a six-month project.

environment in which the employee understands that the supervisor's performance will be evaluated along with his own.

Therefore, the supervisor should learn from the employee how the supervisor can best serve his work-related needs while working on the project. The evaluation session should not only deal with the employee's performance, but also how well the supervisors meet the employee's needs. In most cases the manager should begin the session by asking the employee to identify his work-related needs. Then, they should reach agreement on how these needs can best be met by the supervisor.

Focus on acquiring employee ideas and input. The evaluation session should be a time when the supervisor solicits ideas and input from the employee. This is not necessarily the time for lengthy lectures. The supervisor should first ask the employee for his input concerning the current status of the work, progress being made, problems that have developed since the last meeting, and recommendations for improvements or solutions to problems. This will give the employee an opportunity to use his creativity. It will also communicate that the manager trusts the employee's judgment and needs his input.

Encourage the employee to make decisions within the framework of his authority. Many employees expect the boss to solve all problems and make all decisions concerning changes and other corrective measures. The evaluation session is an excellent time to encourage the employee to solve his own problems as long as the solution falls within the employee's decision-making authority. Don't let the employee delegate problems upward to you when he is capable of developing his own solutions. The manager frequently hinders the employee from taking initiative by stepping in too quickly to rescue the employee from a problem.

If the manager makes the decision for the employee, the employee always has a scapegoat if things don't work out. He can always come back to the supervisor and say, "Your first idea didn't work. How about another one?" On the other hand, if the employee has to make the decisions and solve the problem, he has ownership of the idea and will try harder to make it work because his reputation for ideas and decision-making ability is at stake.

The manager can use the evaluation session to develop the skills of the employee. He can teach the employee to look for better work methods, to make decisions, and to live with the risks involved. The manager who continually makes decisions for his employees is actually doing the work he hired them to do. He is curtailing the creativity of his employees and making them dependent on him.

Use the performance evaluation worksheet to maintain a written record of progress and actions taken. It is very important to keep written records of employee performance. Both progress and problems should be recorded, and the employee should sign the evaluation form at the end of each session. These records provide valuable information when planning similar projects in the future and when it comes time to consider employee promotions.

Always give the proper recognition during the evaluation session. During the evaluation session, the manager should properly recognize the employee's performance. Proper recognition means that the manager offers praise when the job is done well, and constructive criticism when it is needed. Some managers don't mind giving praise, but they don't know how to properly handle constructive criticism.

When dealing with constructive criticism, always focus on performance. Deal with the cause of the performance problem, and never criticize unless you are prepared to offer suggestions for improvement. Stick with facts and try to avoid subjective opinions because they only lead to arguments. It is difficult for an employee to deny poor performance when you deal with facts instead of opinion.

Chapter Summary

Employee performance evaluation is one of the most important tools of management. However, many managers are frustrated with their current evaluation systems because they are designed to evaluate past history instead of work in progress.

Performance evaluation systems that evaluate past history have little if any value because you can't undo past mistakes. On the other hand, evaluation systems applied to work in progress are very beneficial in helping organizations and their employees accomplish projects as planned, thus increasing overall productivity.

Work-in-progress evaluation systems should involve both the supervisor and the employee in the development of measurable objectives, realistic performance standards, and the activities needed to achieve the projects being evaluated.

The evaluation sessions should be conducted in a two-way learning environment. That is, performance of both the supervisor and the subordinate should be evaluated. The supervisor should use the sessions to communicate trust, give decision-making power, turn mistakes into positive learning experiences, and provide proper recognition.

Personal Application

Prepare file folders for each of your employees. Include a sheet of paper with the employee's name, position, title, and department, as outlined in figure 17.

Set up a time to meet with each employee to explain how the work-in-progress performance evaluation system works. This can be done in a group if you have several employees in your department.

Set up a schedule to begin meeting with each employee to start the work-in-progress employee performance evaluation system as outlined in figure 17.

CHAPTER 13

HANDLING ORGANIZATIONAL CONFLICT

Sooner or later every manager or leader finds himself involved either directly or indirectly in some form of organizational conflict. Throughout human history the improper handling of conflicts has destroyed marriages and friendships, dissolved business partnerships and corporations, caused the downfall of great leaders and political empires, and sparked wars.

It is clear then, that conflict is a potentially dangerous phenomenon capable of destroying the effectiveness of any organization or leader. Scripture vividly describes the destructive potential of conflict. "If you keep on biting and devouring each other, watch out or you will be destroyed by each other" (Gal. 5:15).

Ed Hamilton and George Harrison are classic examples of what can happen to people and businesses when conflict is not handled properly.

Several years ago, Ed and George started H and H Manufacturing Company in Ed's garage. They started making small utility trailers for a few friends and before long had developed a backyard business into a highly profitable corporation. The company continued to grow and became one of the largest organizations in the Mid-America city.

However, a few years ago a serious disagreement developed between Ed and George concerning the expansion of their business into the recreational vehicle market. Ed wanted to start manufacturing recreational camp trailers, but George felt the market was saturated and rising fuel prices were decreasing the demand.

The disagreement grew into a serious conflict between the two business partners. They began undermining each other's credibility with fellow employees, and eventually some of their top management personnel resigned to take jobs with major competitors.

As a result, productivity declined and their company began operating in the red. Each partner blamed the other for the decline in business. This led to further conflict, and before long, the corporation was on the verge of bankruptcy.

Recently Ed and George sold what was left of their once profitable and growing business. The Ed Hamiltons moved to Minnesota and the George Harrisons relocated to Colorado.

George told me, "Ed used to be my best friend, but now I consider him my worst enemy. After we sold the business, neither of us could stand to stay in the town where we had known the other—that's why we both moved."

In this chapter we will discuss the various methods people use in dealing with conflict. We will also explore the biblical approach to handling conflict and confrontation.

Defining Organizational Conflict

Conflict can be defined as open and hostile opposition occurring as a result of differing viewpoints. Conflict should not be confused with disagreement. It is possible to have disagreement without hostility. But conflict always involves hostility.

No area of an organization is immune to potential conflict. Open and hostile opposition may develop between individuals, departments, levels of management, and geographic locations. As we saw in H and H Manufacturing, unresolved conflict can lead to the destruction of successful corporations and of close friendships.

The Source of All Organizational Conflict

Conflict comes from our own selfish desires and passions (James 4:1). In a conflict, the emphasis is always on self. We focus on "me" and "mine"—my ideas, my rights, and my feelings.

In Proverbs we read, "Pride only breeds quarrels" (13:10). In a conflict, our conversation is saturated with statements that promote, protect, and draw attention to ourselves. The objective is almost always to impose our ideas, beliefs, desires, and opinions on others.

This was certainly the case with Ed and George. Each became committed to imposing his opinions and beliefs on the other. Both Ed and George were convinced they knew what was best for the company. However, their opposing views grew into open and hostile conflict. Their differing, self-centered viewpoints sparked the hostile conflict between them.

Recently my eighteen-year-old son Ron asked me to help him buy a car. We discussed his need for a car to get to and from work, and I agreed to provide the down payment if he would make the monthly payments and take care of the insurance, maintenance, and incidentals.

The next day he told me he had found a convertible sports car he intended to buy. Would I please provide the money for the down payment as agreed? I felt convertible sports cars were not practical and tried to talk him out of the idea (I began imposing my views and opinions of cars on my son), and soon we were in the midst of a conflict.

I told him I was not willing to provide the down payment unless he bought a "practical" car. He accused me of going back on my word and said I had no right to dictate the type of car he bought as long as he paid for it. I assured him I did have a right to "give input" (a nice term for parents to use then trying to tell older children what to do).

Ron and I had different opinions and each of us tried to impose our views on the other. This resulted in open hostility or conflict.

The Negative Results of Conflict

Conflict causes us to fabricate and magnify faults and weaknesses in others. In the midst of conflict, we seek to justify our position and win the dispute. We are convinced our position is correct; therefore, the other person's position must be wrong. As we set out to "prove" our case, we do so by discrediting the other person's views.

Unfortunately, it is almost impossible to limit negative feelings and thoughts toward others to the issues of the conflict. Instead, we look at other areas of the person's life for additional faults and weaknesses that add support to our feelings and opinions.

For example, a few years ago I found myself in a conflict with my pastor over the lack of lay participation in our Sunday morning worship service. I felt we needed more laymen involved in the worship service. My pastor felt the paid professionals should conduct the activities. As the conflict developed, I became critical of the pastor's sermons, the way he wore his hair, the type of suits he wore on Sunday, and even the way he held his Bible.

I was seeking other faults and weaknesses in my pastor's personality and actions to reinforce my opposing views in our conflict. The more I magnified additional faults and weaknesses, the more hostile toward the pastor I became.

When the issues of the conflict are not kept in focus, we attack the person. This usually results in serious damage to relationships and organizational productivity. Eventually I realized my error, went to my pastor, and asked him to forgive me.

Not long ago I was involved with three other men in a business venture. During a meeting, my friends and I began arguing over the best way to perform a certain task. Before long hostile attitudes formed and we found ourselves in the midst of a serious conflict.

Jerry, the only engineer in our group, tried to explain what should be done from an engineering viewpoint. Soon Bill, a salesman, interrupted, "All of you engineers are alike! You try to snow us with big words and theory, but I've never met one yet who really knew what he was doing!"

Bill had stopped focusing on the issues and was attacking Jerry as a person. This is one of the most detrimental aspects of conflict.

Conflict creates divisions within the organization. Unresolved conflict is the cause of every church split, labor strike, and divorce. Jesus said, "Every kingdom divided against itself will be ruined, and every city or household divided against itself will not stand" (Matt. 12:25).

Division tears both large organizations and individual relationships apart and finally destroys them. In the case of H and H Manufacturing Company, conflict caused division between the owners, Ed and George. As the conflict grew, the division increased until finally it destroyed both their relationship and their successful business.

Conflict causes us to expend our energies on nonproductive activities. Conflict is very detrimental to organizational productivity. Conflict leaves people physically and emotionally drained and consumes a great deal of our "thinking time."

During lunch at a management seminar, a small-business owner told me, "The past couple of weeks I would have accomplished more if I had stayed in bed all day." He explained that he was chairman of his church board and their church was going through a giant conflict over the termination of their minister of music.

"I can't get anything done at work because I'm worrying about what's going to happen at church," he said. "We've had more church board meetings in the past two weeks than in the last eight years combined, and we've accomplished nothing."

When we consider the negative results of conflict on individuals and organizations, it is easy to see why Paul said, "If it is possible, as far as it depends on you, live at peace with everyone" (Rom. 12:18).

The Positive Aspects of Disagreement

Conflict always involves hostility. But it is possible to have disagreement without any ill will. In fact, disagreement can be beneficial.

Disagreement can lead to individual and organizational growth. As figure 20 illustrates, disagreement can lead to individual and organizational changes that ultimately produce improvements.

"As iron sharpens iron, so one man sharpens another" (Prov. 27:17). Two blades of iron can be sharpened by rubbing them together. Likewise, people and organizations grow, develop, and improve by learning to work through disagreements using proper methods of confrontation.

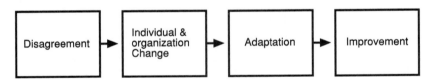

Figure 20. Disagreement can ultimately lead to personal and organizational improvements.

Disagreement can reveal the need for change. The mature leader or manager welcomes disagreement because it forces him to evaluate his own beliefs and to make positive changes where needed.

"The intelligent man is always open to new ideas. In fact, he looks for them" (Prov. 18:15, TLB).

By contrast, the immature leader is defensive, resentful, and hostile when his ideas and opinions are challenged. As a result, the immature leader frequently allows disagreements to erupt into conflicts.

Disagreement can help make us more tolerant of opposing views. Disagreement can become an excellent teacher of tolerance. Learning to accept differing viewpoints without developing hostile reactions is another mark of the mature leader. The effective manager learns to "agree to disagree." He also learns to avoid developing a critical attitude even when others are critical and hostile toward him.

As the leader becomes more tolerant of opposing views, he develops a greater capacity to accept criticism without retaliating. Every leader and manager should learn to apply Proverbs 23:12: "Don't refuse to accept criticism; get all the help you can" (TLB). Unfortunately, most of us don't view criticism as a help, but as a hindrance.

Methods of Dealing with Conflict

There are four basic approaches to dealing with organizational conflict:

- Attempting to avoid conflict by retreating from it

- Attempting to avoid conflict by circumventing the major issues and focusing on minor points

- Attempting to avoid conflict by dealing with side issues

- Identifying the real issues of the conflict and working our way through them to a satisfactory resolution

Notice that three of these approaches focus on attempting to avoid the real problem. Unfortunately, many managers spend more time attempting to avoid a conflict than trying to face the issues and resolve them.

Attempting to avoid conflict by retreating from it. Many leaders tend to run from an existing conflict. There are many ways to do this. Most attempts take the form of procrastination. The leader simply delays dealing with the problem.

Once a conflict develops, it can never be solved by retreating or avoiding the issues involved. In fact, the longer we avoid dealing with the conflict, the worse it becomes.

Earlier I pointed out that my son Ron and I had developed a conflict over the type of car he wanted to buy. The problem erupted one evening at the dinner table and the verbal battle continued through most of the evening.

During the next several days, I tried to avoid the issue. On numerous occasions Ron approached me with the subject, and each time I found some excuse for delaying the matter. With each delay I could see that Ron was becoming more upset. And the more hostile he became, the more determined I was not to back down from my demand that I influence the type of car he bought, since I was making the down payment.

The longer we delayed dealing with the problem, the more hostile each of us became. This is usually the pattern that appears when people develop a conflict, then refuse to deal with the issues.

Ironically, I procrastinated in dealing with the conflict because I wanted to avoid future hostile discussions with my son. However, the longer I avoided the situation, the more hostile we both became.

Betty Owens, the head of a large, multicounty Head Start project, developed a serious conflict with Joan, her coordinator of social services, over Joan's work schedule. At the beginning of the program year, Betty conducted an orientation session with her staff and explained the importance of each office employee maintaining regularly scheduled office hours.

A few weeks later, some of the office staff complained to Betty that Joan was not spending much time in the office and wasn't maintaining an office schedule.

When Betty approached Joan with the complaint, Joan became angry. She was involved in numerous evening meetings with parents and other people in the community. She therefore felt she should not be required to check in at the office every morning like the rest of the staff. On the other hand, Betty felt the salary Joan made more than compensated for the time spent in additional evening meetings and that Joan should keep daily office hours like everyone else.

The conflict was not resolved during the meeting; after that, Betty tried to avoid the issue. However, the other staff members continued to remind Betty that Joan still did not keep regular office hours. When they saw that Betty was avoiding the issue, they became upset and accused her of showing favoritism. A short time later, one of Betty's best staff members resigned and went to work for another organization because of Betty's failure to resolve the conflict with Joan.

Betty's problem with Joan is a classic example of what happens when we procrastinate in dealing with conflict. Betty's failure to resolve the problem not only created poor morale within the office, but caused her to lose a good employee.

Attempting to avoid conflict by dealing with the minor issues involved and circumventing the real ones. Some managers and leaders approach a conflict by talking their way around the important issues and dealing only with the minor ones.

During my conflict with Ron concerning the type of car he should buy, I tried to focus on a "practical" car according to my definition. I tried to point out the importance of buying a car that would be easy to maintain and cheap to operate. And I tried to convince Ron I was upset with his choice because a sports car would be expensive to run. He pointed out that he would be paying the operating expenses, not me. Therefore, he couldn't understand why I would not approve of the car. It seemed obvious to him I had other reasons to oppose his choice.

When we try to limit our discussions to the minor points of the conflict, we make those involved more upset and frustrated. They soon recognize we are not being honest and are avoiding the real issues.

This happened with Ron. He realized I wasn't leveling with him and became more hostile, accusing me of not wanting him to have a car at all.

What was my real reason for not wanting him to have the sports car? I feared it would present an added temptation to race and increase his risk of a serious accident. However, I didn't want him to think I couldn't trust his maturity behind the wheel of a car, so I tried to focus on other issues of minor importance.

As long as we limit our focus to minor points of the conflict, there is no chance for resolution. We must be willing to honestly state the real issues involved.

Attempting to avoid conflict by dealing with side issues. This is one of the most dangerous methods of trying to deal with conflict because it almost always creates additional problems.

Dealing with side issues is usually an attempt to divert attention away from the conflict. However, it frequently leads to additional conflicts because the hostility associated with the conflict creates a climate of confusion and misunderstanding in any communication or discussion.

Herbert Brixey owns and operates a heavy equipment repair business. His shop foreman, Gary Green, hired his own son Walter as a heavy equipment mechanic and started him out at the top of the salary scale.

The other employees heard what Walter was making and complained to Herbert about the shop foreman's favoritism toward his son. Finally, Herbert decided he had to confront his shop foreman with the problem. However, Gary had been a good supervisor for so many years that Herbert didn't want to upset him and possibly cause him to quit.

One day Herbert took Gary to lunch and, in an effort to point out that Walter was being paid too much, started criticizing Walter's lack of experience. Immediately Gary became defensive. He told

Herbert that Walter had far more experience as a mechanic than Herbert's daughter had as an accountant working in the office.

Before long each man was accusing the other of favoritism and poor judgment in hiring people. As a result, both Gary and his son quit.

Instead of focusing on the employees' feelings over Walter's salary, Herbert dealt with a side issue involving Walter's lack of experience. As a result, he created a bigger problem than if he had dealt with the source of the real conflict.

Identifying the real issues of the conflict and working our way through them to a satisfactory resolution. The only way to resolve a conflict is to approach it head on, identify the issues involved, and work your way through them.

A few days following the development of my conflict with my son Ron over his car, I sat down with him and apologized for being angry about his choice of a car. I explained my concerns for his safety and told him my real reasons for not wanting him to buy a sports car.

I also admitted I couldn't continue to treat him like a child and agreed to trust his judgment in choosing the right car. I assured him I would be willing to provide the down payment on the car he chose.

A couple of days later he decided on a Volkswagen "Bug." As we drove to the courthouse to get it licensed, he said, "You know, Dad, as soon as you were willing to let me pick the car I wanted, I realized I didn't really want a gas-guzzling sports car." He smiled and said, "If we'd talked like this in the beginning, I could have been driving my car days ago."

In dealing with conflict we must be willing to be honest with the others involved and clearly state the real issues. We must also be willing to ask forgiveness for the hostility we feel toward the other persons. And we must be willing to trust the others involved to make decisions that will be in the best interests of everyone concerned with the conflict.

We should never procrastinate in dealing with a conflict. As long as conflict exists we are harboring hostility toward others. This violates the Scriptures, which tell us, "Don't let the sun go down with you still angry—get over it quickly; for when you are angry you give a mighty foothold to the Devil" (Eph. 4:26-27, TLB).

A Scriptural Approach to Handling Confrontation

Many leaders and managers are afraid to deal with conflict because it involves confrontation. However, by confrontation, we don't mean dispute. Anyone can get involved in a dispute or an argument, but it takes a mature person to handle confrontation properly. The Bible gives the Christian leader and manager a step-by-step process for handling confrontation successfully.

First, make sure you are dealing with facts, not guesses or hearsay. "Never convict anyone on the testimony of one witness. There must be at least two, and three is even better" (Deut. 19:15, TLB).

This passage gives us a very important principle for dealing with confrontation. We must make sure we are operating on facts, not hearsay or opinion. This is the first and most important principle of confrontation. Operating on hearsay or assumptions usually insures failure when trying to deal with conflict. Unless the confrontation focuses on facts, it degenerates to one opinion versus another.

Second, always make the initial confrontation in private between you and the person involved. "Discuss the matter with him privately. Don't tell anyone else, lest he accuse you of slander" (Prov. 25:9-10, TLB). Matthew 18:15 in the Phillips version reads, "But if your brother wrongs you, go and have it out with him at once—just between the two of you."

Every effort should be made to resolve the conflict in private with those involved. Many leaders make the mistake of publicly criticizing others involved in a conflict. This only compounds the problems and undermines people's trust. The Bible makes it clear that those involved in the conflict should keep the confrontation a private matter.

Third, when you try to resolve the conflict privately, if the other person involved refuses to resolve the problem, take someone with you and try again. "But if he will not listen to you, take one or two others with you so that everything that is said may have the support of two or three witnesses" (Matt. 18:16, PH).

This is an important principle of confrontation. Involve others only after you are convinced the other person refuses to listen to you. At this point, outside help in resolving the conflict does two things. First, it allows a neutral party to provide input into resolving the problem. Secondly, it gives evidence to others that you are honestly trying to resolve the problem.

Fourth, if the person continues to resist resolving the conflict, you may need to dissolve the relationship. Once we have done everything in our power to resolve the problem but the other person refuses to cooperate in correcting the situation, the relationship should be terminated (see Matt. 18:17).

On the other hand, as long as the other person is willing to repent and correct the problem, you are obligated to forgive and continue the relationship—no matter how often conflicts continue to occur. "If your brother sins, rebuke him, and if he repents, forgive him. If he sins against you seven times in a day, and seven times comes back to you and says, 'I repent,' forgive him" (Luke 17:3).

When dealing with confrontation we should keep in mind Proverbs 20:3. "It is to a man's honor to avoid strife, but every fool is quick to quarrel." Conflict should be avoided whenever possible, but when it exists it should not be ignored. We should confront those involved with the facts and privately work at resolving the problem.

When dealing with confrontation, keep the following points in mind:

1. *A conflict provides an excellent opportunity to serve others.* Jesus said, "If someone wants to sue you and take your tunic, let him have your cloak as well. If someone forces you to go one mile, go with him two miles" (Matt. 5:40-41). Be sensitive to the needs of others instead of demanding your own way.

Jerry Marshall, a friend and business partner of mine, once told me, "When doing good costs us nothing, we are more than willing to do it. But the more it costs, the more we resist." A conflict provides an excellent opportunity to do good to others.

2. *Be committed to resolving the conflict quickly.* The longer the conflict continues, the more difficult it is to resolve.

3. *Take the initiative in confronting those involved.* Don't wait for them to come to you. Jesus touched on this idea when He said, "If your brother wrongs you, go and have it out with him at once" (Matt. 18:15, PH).

4. *Even though hostility and anger are present in conflict, avoid angry arguments.* "A patient man has great understanding, but a quick-tempered man displays folly" (Prov. 14:29). If we display anger during a confrontation, we stimulate anger in others. On the other hand, if we control our emotions during the confrontation, we ease the tension and anger in those involved. This will make it easier to find a satisfactory solution.

Chapter Summary

No one is immune to conflict. Eventually every leader and manager becomes involved in some form of organizational conflict. We can define conflict as open and hostile opposition occurring as a result of differing viewpoints.

During a conflict, the emphasis is always on self. We tend to promote our desires, wishes, and opinions while criticizing those of others involved in the problem.

Conflict always produces negative results for individuals and organizations. For example, it causes us to fabricate and magnify faults and weaknesses in others; it creates divisions within an organization; and it causes us to spend our energies and efforts on nonproductive activities.

On the other hand, disagreements that lack hostility can be beneficial to people and organizations. Disagreement can produce individual and organizational growth; make us aware of the need for change; and make us more tolerant of opposing views.

People use various methods to deal with conflict. Some try to avoid conflict by retreating or procrastinating in dealing with the real issues. Some individuals try to focus on the minor issues and avoid the real source of the conflict. Others try to focus on side issues actually unrelated to the problem. None of these approaches works, and they usually increase the problem instead of resolving it.

The proper way to deal with conflict is to approach it head-on, identify the real issues involved, and work your way through them to a satisfactory conclusion. However, this approach requires the leader to be able to handle confrontation properly.

In dealing with confrontation, first make sure you have the facts and are not operating on assumptions. Also, try to resolve the problem privately with only those involved in the conflict. If it is impossible to resolve the conflict with those involved, seek outside, neutral assistance.

Always keep in mind that conflict provides an excellent opportunity to serve those involved in the problem. And be committed to resolving the conflict quickly. The longer the conflict drags on, the more difficult it is to develop satisfactory solutions. Also, take the initiative in confronting those involved; don't wait for them to come to you. And finally, keep your emotions under control. Remember, hostility is always present in conflict. The more hostility you display, the more angry and hostile the others involved will become.

Personal Application

With the help of your staff or peers, evaluate the organization for areas of potential conflict.

Begin developing solutions and taking corrective actions now. Don't wait for the conflict to materialize.

If you are currently involved in a conflict, apply the principles of confrontation outlined in this chapter.

Make sure your actions demonstrate a spirit of love, not anger and hostility.

CHAPTER 14

AN EFFECTIVE LEADERSHIP STYLE

What role does leadership and management style play in determining an organization's success and productivity? That question has been the subject of numerous discussions, debates, and lectures within leadership and management circles during the past several years. I have observed that management style exerts an important influence on how organizations function and their level of productivity.

Keeping Leadership's Role in Focus

Ezekiel 34 provides an excellent example of how leadership style and attitude impact people and organizational productivity:

Woe to the shepherds of Israel who only take care of themselves! Should not shepherds take care of the flock? You eat the curds, clothe yourselves with the wool and slaughter the choice animals, but you do not take care of the flock. You have not strengthened the weak or healed the sick or bound up the injured. You have not brought back the strays or searched for the lost. You have ruled them harshly and brutally. So they were scattered because there was no shepherd (vv. 2-5).

Some very important leadership principles are suggested here.

The leader should not exploit those who work under him. To pursue our own selfish interests while neglecting the needs of the people who serve under us is offensive to God. He pronounces a "woe" on any such style of leadership.

The leader should look for ways to serve those under him. People have lots of needs to be met. The weak need to be strengthened and encouraged. The sick need to be healed. The strays need to be brought back. The lost need to be found. Israel's leaders in Ezekiel's time did not meet any of these needs. On the contrary, they used their power to be cruel and harsh with the people. Keep in mind that the effective leader uses his position and authority to serve the needs of others, not to force them to serve his needs.

The good leader or manager is constantly looking for ways to help his people—to make their jobs easier, more meaningful, more satisfying, and more productive.

The leader should serve willingly and eagerly. "Be shepherds of God's flock that is under your care, serving as overseers—not because you must, but because you are willing, as God wants you to be" (1 Peter 5:2). The effective leader does not complain about his responsibility to serve the work-related needs of subordinates.

The leader should exhibit such a spirit that people willingly follow. We saw from Ezekiel that the leaders used their positions to meet their own needs and desires at their people's expense. In addition, they had behaved "harshly and brutally," with the effect on the people being, "So they were scattered because there was no shepherd"(34:5).

Notice that the excessive use of authority and failure to meet the people's needs drove them away. This principle applies to the church on the corner as well as to the factory down the street. People resist the excessive use of authority by their leaders.

The New Testament tells us to avoid dominating those under us. "Not lording it over those entrusted to you, but being examples to the flock" (1 Peter 5:3). Leaders are to provide an example people will want to follow. How do they do that? As mentioned in Chapter 1, "If today you will be a servant to these people and serve them and give them a favorable answer, they will always be your servants" (1 Kings 12:7). People will serve and follow the leader who first serves their needs.

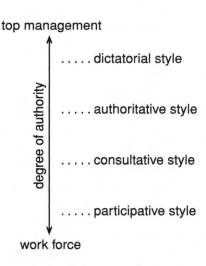

Figure 21. The amount of authority divided between top management and the work force helps determine the type of leadership style being used.

The Key Ingredients of Leadership Style

Leadership style focuses on how you use authority. As figure 21 illustrates, authority plays an important role in determining the type of leadership style being used.

In Exodus 18 Moses transferred his authority, or decision-making power, to newly appointed leaders under him.

At first Moses was a very authoritative leader, making almost all important decisions for the people (vv. 13-16). Through the counsel of his father-in-law, Moses became aware of the need to transfer some of his authority to other leaders who would answer to him (vv. 17-22). In the leadership style that emerged, Moses delegated to others most of his authority affecting the day-to-day operations of the nation (vv. 24-26).

The amount of authority you retain and the type of decisions you make for your people play a major role in determining your leadership style. Therefore, if you want to determine your leadership style, look at the way you use authority. Do you make most of the decisions for your people? Or do you delegate substantial decision-making power to those under you?

Leadership style influences how you use human resources. Some leadership styles encourage and promote employee involvement in planning, problem-solving, and decision-making. Others tend to limit employee involvement in these areas.

As a general rule, the more authoritative you are, the less you are willing to use the creative ideas of others. You use people's muscles instead of their minds.

Leadership style affects how you relate to people. The more authoritative the leadership style, the more the leader or manager separates himself from his people. Some leadership styles promote the concept that people work for you. Others project the idea that you work with the people.

Leadership style also influences the type of communication that develops between leadership and the workforce. The more authoritative the style, the more communication tends to be one-way—from the top down. Communication focuses on telling and giving information in the more authoritative leadership styles.

However, as employees are given more authority and as the leader works with the people, communication becomes a two-way process. Leaders begin asking for more input instead of always giving instructions.

The Types of Leadership Styles

Definitions and descriptions of leadership styles range from the simple to the complex. However, we will focus on a practical approach to leadership styles and provide a simple tool to help you determine the leadership styles in your organization.

Leadership styles can be identified and categorized according to the way authority is used, how people's minds and muscles are used, and how the leader relates to and communicates with those under him. The four styles of leadership listed in figure 21 are:

- Dictatorial style

- Authoritative style

- Consultative style

- Participative team style

The Dictatorial Style

As the name indicates, the leader or manager using this style of leadership operates like a dictator. He makes all decisions concerning what, when, where, and how things are done and who will do them. People failing to carry out his instructions are usually severely disciplined.

Daniel 2:1-13 provides a classic example of the dictatorial style of leadership in action. King Nebuchadnezzar had a dream and commanded his wise men to explain it to him, even though he had forgotten what it was about. When Nebuchadnezzar's magicians and enchanters said that he was making an unrealistic and unfair demand, he became furious and told them they would be killed if they didn't tell him the dream and its meaning.

The dictatorial leader manifests the following traits:

- Keeps all decision-making power for himself

- Is frequently unrealistic in his work demands, asking people to do the impossible

- Often uses excessive discipline and punishment on those failing to carry out instructions to his satisfaction

- Does not allow people to question his decisions or authority

The Authoritative Style

Few leaders and managers consistently operate from a dictatorial style of leadership. However, many people do adopt the authoritative style.

Saul, Israel's first king, provides an interesting case study of an authoritative leader in action. Saul was a very decisive leader, using his position and authority to motivate people to follow him into battle (1 Sam. 11). However, he soon overstepped his authority by performing priestly sacrifices (chap. 13). Later, his quick decisions and pride almost caused the death of his son Jonathan (chap. 14).

Saul was willing to receive help from a lad when it was to his advantage and benefit (chap. 17), but he generally acted as an authoritative leader unwilling to let anyone else share in his power and position (chaps. 18–27).

The authoritative leader displays the following characteristics:

- Seldom lets others make decisions because he feels his experience and expertise make him the most qualified

- Considers his views to be the most valid

- Is frequently critical of opinions and decisions that differ from his own

- Frequently lacks confidence in other people's ability

- Rarely gives his employees recognition for a job well done

- Will apply other people's ideas only if he agrees with them

- Is offended if other people disagree with his point of view

- Frequently uses others for his own benefit

- Is frequently action-oriented and highly competitive

The authoritative leader's biggest weakness is his failure to recognize the skills and abilities of his people. He denies them opportunity to use their skills in planning and decision-making. On the other hand, his greatest strength is his ability to produce action when needed.

The Consultative Style

The consultative style of leadership focuses on using the skills and ideas of others in formulating plans and making decisions. For the most part, the leader using this style of leadership still retains final decision-making power. However, he does not make major decisions without first seeking input from those affected by the decisions.

Acts 6:1-7 provides an excellent example of the consultative leadership style in action. As the church grew, some people's needs were no longer being met (a problem growing churches have today).

When the Grecian Jews pointed out that some of their widows were being neglected, the 12 Apostles told them to choose seven men they could appoint to serve the widow's needs. This passage suggests several excellent leadership principles that clearly demonstrate the consultative leadership style.

First, the leaders had the people with the problem work on the solution. The consultative style of leadership always attempts to involve those who have a problem in seeking ideas for the solution. This helps develop leadership and decision-making ability in them.

Second, the leaders had the people work together on the problem. The consultative leadership style focuses on building a team. People learn to work together and use their strengths in focusing on a project.

Third, the leaders reserved the right to review the work and make the final decisions. In this style of leadership other people's ideas are solicited and used, but the leader still retains final decision-making power.

Fourth, the leaders were able to work on other important projects while information was being gathered to solve the widows' problem. This is a major strength of consultative leadership. By involving other people in planning and problem-solving activities, the leader frees his time to concentrate on more important aspects of his job.

The consultative leader:

- Asks for input from subordinates on a regular basis

- Never makes major decisions without getting input from those being affected by the decision

- Works at providing proper recognition

- Is willing to delegate certain decision-making responsibility, but retains veto power

- Attempts to weigh all alternatives suggested before making a decision, and then explains why certain ideas were not used

The Participative Team Style

This is a unique leadership style and many managers feel uncomfortable using it. In this style of leadership, the manager gives most of his authority—but not all of it—to his team. However, he remains the team's leader.

This leadership style displays the following traits:

- Members of the team are considered equal with the leader in terms of input and ideas. This means everyone's ideas are considered equally

- The leader assumes the role of a player/coach and becomes the team's facilitator

- The leader frequently—but not always—accepts the team's ideas, even when they disagree with his own

- The leader focuses on stimulating creativity and innovation within the team

There Is Not a "Right" Leadership Style

Most management trainers and consultants tend to promote one leadership style as being the right style of leadership. The good manager or leader learns how and when to use each of the leadership styles discussed in this chapter.

Jesus used various leadership styles depending on the situation He faced. He used a dictatorial style when driving the money changers out of the temple (John 2:13-16).

It might seem that this was not an act of leadership as such, since those Jesus evicted were not His followers. However, as Jesus said at the time, they were desecrating His Father's house (v. 16). Therefore, it was His business to respond and the situation called for immediate strong action, not for consultation either between Jesus and His disciples or between Jesus and the money changers.

However, in other situations, we see Jesus making the disciples part of His team. He gave them authority to perform many of the tasks He had been doing in the various villages He visited (Matt. 10:1-15). We see, then, that Jesus was a leader Who knew how and when to use the various leadership styles to accomplish the job most effectively. We would do well to follow His example.

When to Use the Leadership Styles

Dictatorial leadership is appropriate:

- During extreme emergencies or crises, when people's safety is at stake

- When severe disciplinary action is required

The leader should keep in mind that this style of leadership represents the exception to the rule, and should be used only in emergencies and on a temporary basis.

The authoritative leadership style is appropriate:

- When employees consistently misuse authority

- With new employees unfamiliar with the details of their jobs

- When organizational rules and regulations are violated

- When you are solely responsible for making and carrying out a decision

The consultative leadership style is appropriate:

- In conducting ongoing planning for the department or organization

- When creative problem-solving is needed

- In training people to assume leadership responsibilities

- When performing many of the day-to-day organizational functions and tasks

The participative team style is appropriate:

- As people become competent in performing their routine responsibilities

- During organizational planning sessions

- During organizational evaluation sessions

- When you need to continue to motivate highly qualified people, who tend to become stifled in their routine assignments

- Anytime there is a need for highly creative and innovative work

How Leadership Style Impacts Productivity

There are short-term and long-term effects of the various leadership styles. Over a short span of time, an authoritative style of leadership may produce the greatest results. However, as a general rule, excessive use of authority tends to decrease organizational productivity over a long period of time.

On the other hand, a participative team leadership style tends to be unproductive over a short period of time. However, the longer this style of leadership is in place, the more productive it becomes.

The leader should not become discouraged if there is an initial drop in productivity as he changes his style to a more participative approach. Productivity starts low but becomes greater as people have an opportunity to work with a participative team style of leadership.

Unfortunately, many managers are not willing to give the participative team style of leadership a chance to stabilize because they experience an initial decline in productivity. But over the long span of time, it offers the best approach to developing a highly productive organization.

Plotting Your Organization's Leadership Style

The following form is designed to help leaders and organizations determine their leadership style. For best results, the form should be filled out by all employees at least annually to determine if the organization's leadership style is changing.

Administering the form shown in figure 22 is an ideal way for a leader to identify his leadership style. Record the average scores on a master form and connect those scores with a solid line. By doing this year after year, you can keep track of the organization's leadership

INSTRUCTIONS.
Place an N at the pint in which, in your experience, describes your organization at the present time (N-now). In addition, if you have been in your organization a year or more, place a P on each line at the point which, in your experience, describes your organization as it was previously (P-previously). If you were not in your organization a year ago, please check here _____.

	system 1	system 2	system 3	system 4

PLANNING
Subordinates are involved in the planning process:

rarely	some	frequently	always

The amount of covert resistance to goals is:

strong	moderate	occasional	almost none

The number of employees who know the organization's plans is:

almost none	relatively few	most	almost all

Planning occurs:

mostly at top	top and middle	fairly general	at all levels

MOTIVATION
Subordinates feel they are not trusted.

in most cases	frequently	occasionally	rarely

Subordinates have decision-making power withing their job frame.

almost none	some	usually	always

Subordinates feel ownership in plans.

rarely	occasionally	frequently	always

Employees receive recognition for work.

almost none	some	usually	always

COMMUNICATION
Subordinates feel free to offer suggestions and point out problems.

rarely	occasionally	usually	almost always

Superiors know the working needs and problems of subordinates.

not very well	rather well	quite well	very well

Information is exchanged between departments.

not very well	rather well	quite well	very well

Information received from others is:

rarely accurate	usually accurate	mostly accurate	very accurate

RESOURCE UTILIZATION
Superiors ask subordinates for their ideas.

rarely	occasionally	usually	almost always

Solutions to common problems are shared between projects or departments.

almost never	once in a while	usually	almost always

Authority for problem-solving is delegated downward:	almost never	when necessary	frequently	whenever possible

Coordination of equipment material and supply usage is:	very poor	poor	satisfactory	good

Duplication of effort is:	regular	occasional	seldom	almost never

Effective teamwork is:	rare	occasional	frequent	almost always

CONTROL

Time spent correcting mistakes is:	much	substantial	some	very little

Effort spent identifying and removing hidden costs is:	ignored	seldom considered	often considered	usually considered

Focus on control functions is at:	top only	top/middle	some lower levels	widely shared

RELATIONSHIPS

Relationships between superiors and subordinates are good:	rarely	occasionally	usually	almost always

Relationships between departments are good:	rarely	occasionally	usually	almost always

Conflict tends to occur:	always	frequently	occasionally	rarely

The attitude toward authority is:	very bad	poor	average	quite good

Conflict is quickly resolved:	rarely	occasionally	usually	almost always

Employees live in fear of failure:	almost always	usually	occasionally	rarely

Employees tend to have a positive mental attitude toward the organization.	rarely	occasionally	usually	almost always

	top management	middle management	supervisor	non-supervisor

I am the following type of employee:

_____ _____ _____ _____

Figure 22. Use this chart to plot your organizational leadership style.

221

INSTRUCTIONS.
Place an N at the pint in which, in your experience, describes your organization at the present time (N-now). In addition, if you have been in your organization a year or more, place a P on each line at the point which, in your experience, describes your organization as it was previously (P-previously). If you were not in your organization a year ago, please check here _____.

	system 1	system 2	system 3	system 4
PLANNING Subordinates are involved in the planning process:	rarely	some	frequently	always
The amount of covert resistance to goals is:	strong	moderate	occasional	almost none
The number of employees who know the organization's plans is:	almost none	relatively few	most	almost all
Planning occurs:	mostly at top	top and middle	fairly general	at all levels
MOTIVATION Subordinates feel they are not trusted.	in most cases	frequently	occasionally	rarely
Subordinates have decision-making power within their job frame.	almost none	some	usually	always
Subordinates feel ownership in plans.	rarely	occasionally	frequently	always
Employees receive recognition for work.	almost none	some	usually	always

Figure 23. By plotting each year's results, an organization can keep track of it's progress toward a participative team leadership style.

development toward a more participative team leadership style (see fig. 23).

The form is coded as follows:

System 1 = Dictatorial leadership style

System 2 = Authoritative leadership style

System 3 = Consultative leadership style

System 4 = Participative team leadership style

It is best to leave these systems unidentified on the form to be filled out in order to avoid "programming" people's response in a certain column.

The leader should keep in mind that there are times when each of these styles should be used. However, for the most part, he should be working to establish a more consultative or participative team style in order to promote long-term increased productivity.

If you decide to have your employees fill out the organizational leadership style form, be sure to share the results with them. People feel they are being taken advantage of when they are asked to give input but are never told the results.

Chapter Summary

The leader should keep in mind that leadership style plays a major role in determining organizational productivity. He should also remember that the leader's job is to serve the work-related needs of those under him.

Three key ingredients greatly influence leadership style: how you use your authority, how you view human resources, and how you relate to people.

The more you hang on to decision-making power, the more authoritative your leadership style. The more you share authority with others, using their minds in place of their muscle, and the more you allow them to become involved in the planning and problem-solving processes, the more you move toward a participative team style of leadership.

There are four styles of leadership: dictatorial, authoritative, consultative, and participative team. There is no "right" style for all occasions. The effective leader learns how and when to use each style. However, as a general rule, the more you move toward a participative team style, the more productive you and your people become.

Personal Application

Have people fill out the form, "Plotting Your Organization's Leadership Style" (fig. 22).

Plot the averages on a master form as shown in figure 23.

Share the results with your people. This can be done in several ways, either in large or small groups.

Ask your people for input on how to improve in the areas that indicate improvement is needed.

Repeat the administering of the form annually.

CHAPTER 15

THE CHRISTIAN MANAGER'S ROLE IN SOCIETY

Recently I was having lunch with a non-Christian friend. He began telling me how a well-known Christian businessman in our community had cheated another person out of a piece of property. As we discussed the incident, he said, "Myron, I sort of expect that kind of action from my friends, but it really shocks me when you churchgoers pull something like that!"

I flinched at his statement, but tried not to show my frustration. I had to admit my friend was right. It should shock all of us if the Christian businessperson or leader operates no differently than an unprincipled non-Christian.

As I drove back to my office following lunch with my friend, I thought of the Scripture that says, "In everything set them an example by doing what is good . . . So that those who oppose you may be ashamed because they have nothing bad to say about us," (Titus 2:7-8).

I must confess that as I travel across this country working with secular as well as Christian organizations, I hear numerous comments similar to the one made by my non-Christian friend. Too many of us have forgotten the important admonition of Titus 2:7-8.

The non-Christian people in the marketplaces of the world develop their opinions of Jesus Christ and His church by observing Christians as they perform their day-to-day responsibilities. They neither know nor care how we act on Sunday morning inside the four walls of the church building. Therefore, the Christian leader and businessperson is playing a key role in influencing modern society's attitude and opinion of Christianity and Jesus Christ.

A church in one of our northern states decided to construct a new building. They raised money and let subcontracts. However, the project cost more than they had planned, and they did not have enough money to pay all of their subcontractors.

Instead of borrowing the money, they tried to get the subcontractors to lower their prices. One of the subcontractors told me, "I had four meetings with the church board trying to get the money they owed me, but they never paid." He was not a Christian, and he used very descriptive language as he recalled the incident. "I learned one thing from that experience," he said with a curse: "I'll never bid on another church building because those Christians don't keep their word or pay their bills."

Carl McCutchan, an engineer who several years ago led me to Jesus Christ, used to tell me, "Myron, it's not what you say you do but what you actually do that communicates what you really are." I have never forgotten that bit of wisdom from my dear friend and spiritual father.

"Don't copy the behavior and customs of this world, but be a new and different person with a fresh newness in all you do and think. Then you will learn from your own experience how His ways will really satisfy you" (Rom. 12:2, TLB). Every leader and manager calling himself a Christian should memorize that verse and work at applying it daily.

As a leader or manager, you constantly have opportunities to "copy the behavior and customs of this world" as you perform your day-to-day tasks and functions. One of the most important decisions you make each day is whether to conform to the world's humanistic standard of business ethics or to follow God's principles of dealing with our fellow man. I trust this book has, in some way, stimulated you to apply more conscientiously the various biblical principles of management we have discussed in the preceding chapters.

As we have already indicated, you play an important role in shaping society and its receptivity to Jesus Christ. Therefore, you should strive to be an effective example as a leader or businessperson in your community by applying God's Word to your daily work. In doing so, you will discover Christians and non-Christians alike will be encouraged to give praise to God.

How a Christian's faithfulness can bring praise to God even from a non-Christian is illustrated by the visit of the queen of Sheba to King Solomon. "When the queen of Sheba heard about the fame of Solomon and his relation to the name of the Lord, she came to test him with hard questions" (1 Kings 10:1).

Notice that the queen of Sheba heard both about King Solomon's fame and his relationship to the Lord. People soon become aware when a person consistently applies God's Word to his daily life.

> When the queen of Sheba saw all the wisdom of Solomon and the palace he had built, the food on his table, the seating of his officials, the attending servants in their robes, his cupbearers, and the burnt offerings he made at the temple of the Lord, she was overwhelmed. She said to the king, "The report I heard in my own county about your achievements and your wisdom is true . . . Praise be to the Lord your God" (1 Kings 10:4-9).

Notice the queen had heard reports of how Solomon conducted his affairs even in her own land. And when she observed his actions for herself—the way he conducted his affairs and applied God's Word to his day-to-day life—she gave praise to God.

People are watching your life—how you conduct your daily business activities—and they are either praising God like the queen of

Sheba, or they are shocked because you are no different from the rest of society.

My prayer is that you and your organization or business will become more effective and productive as a result of reading this. May your example as a leader stimulate other leaders, managers, and businesspeople—Christians and non-Christians alike—to turn to God's Word for direction in their own daily leadership and business practices.

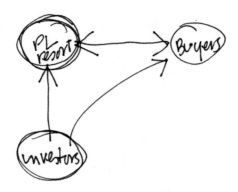

Team   · Recognition

PIERRE   · Trust   PETE   DR
                                        consub
JB   ·   OMAR   ALEX

ALAIN   TONY

LC MILES   RALPH

REDD

CLARK

EKEL   Planning

PIERRE   What is Warranted?
JB   responsible?
ROLAND
STEFAN

PETE